TOWN SWAMPS
AND
SOCIAL BRIDGES

THE VICTORIAN LIBRARY

TOWN SWAMPS
AND
SOCIAL BRIDGES

GEORGE GODWIN

WITH AN INTRODUCTION BY
ANTHONY D. KING

LEICESTER UNIVERSITY PRESS
NEW YORK: HUMANITIES PRESS
1972

First published in volume form in 1859
Victorian Library edition published in 1972 by
Leicester University Press

Distributed in North America by
Humanities Press Inc., New York

Introduction copyright © Leicester University Press 1972

Printed in Great Britain by
Unwin Brothers Ltd, Old Woking, Surrey
Introduction set in Monotype Modern Extended 7

ISBN 0 7185 5014 5

THE VICTORIAN LIBRARY

There is a growing demand for the classics of Victorian literature in many fields, in political and social history, architecture, topography, religion, education, and science. Hitherto this demand has been met, in the main, from the second-hand market. But the prices of second-hand books are rising sharply, and the supply of them is very uncertain. It is the object of this series, THE VICTORIAN LIBRARY, to make some of these classics available again at a reasonable cost. Since most of the volumes in it are reprinted photographically from the first edition, or another chosen because it has some special value, an accurate text is ensured. Each work carries a substantial introduction, written specially for this series by a well-known authority on the author or his subject, and a bibliographical note on the text.

The volumes necessarily vary in size. In planning the newly-set pages the designer, Arthur Lockwood, has maintained a consistent style for the principal features. The uniform design of binding and jackets provides for ready recognition of the various books in the series when shelved under different subject classifications.

Recommendation of titles for THE VICTORIAN LIBRARY and of scholars to contribute the introductions is made by a joint committee of the Board of the University Press and the Victorian Studies Centre of the University of Leicester.

INTRODUCTION

I

In the century and more since this work was first published, its theme has been of continuing concern to all industrializing and modernizing societies: how can strains on the social, economic and political fabric, generated by rapid urbanization, be contained or eradicated? Though the theme is familiar the title is specific to its own age and culture; what Godwin described in 1859 as *Town Swamps and Social Bridges* would appear today as *Urban Poverty and the Role of Voluntary Action*. Instead of the emotion-charged journalism typical of mid-nineteenth century England[1] there would be an appropriate theoretical framework, empirical research and an action-oriented programme for planned change.

Yet the same kind of questions, basic for an understanding of a book on such a theme, would be likely to remain unanswered: what motivates the author's concern, his dissatisfaction with the status quo? What societal or cultural characteristics does he assume in the solutions he suggests? What particular set of values distinguishes him from the system he sees fit to criticize and, of equal importance, what set of values nonetheless prevents him from proposing solutions outside the boundaries of that system? Answers to these queries are as important for an understanding of Godwin's role in nineteenth-century urban reform in England as they are for an insight into contemporary programmes of urban development in more distant regions of the world. Only some of these issues will be touched on here.

Godwin's book represents his second collection of writings previously published in his journal, *The Builder*. The first, *London Shadows: A Glance at the Homes of the Thousands*, had appeared in 1854; *Another Blow for Life* was to follow in 1864. Any appreciation of their significance might consider at least three distinct but interrelated frames of reference, drawn from social and intellectual history, urban sociology and studies in modernization and development.

For the historical context of nineteenth-century urban reform in England, it is not necessary to repeat what Anthony Wohl has written in his introduction to an earlier volume in the Victorian Library series.[2] The period between the 1830s and the 1890s is commonly accepted as a significant era in British social and cultural development. It was a transitional era embodying growing concern, at first individual and then public, initially with urban poverty, then with sanitation and finally, with the manifest need for public if not mass housing, each stage of the transition being marked by a realization of the links which existed between them. Godwin's writings form part of this historical process and help to establish his reputation as a major figure in Victorian urban development.

Yet these works can be seen in a second context. Godwin was one of the earlier, lesser-known contributors to the "large pioneering literature of empirical sociology" which helped to establish the nineteenth-century origin of English urban studies. It was a literature which, as others have pointed out, combined fact-finding and analysis with protest, comment and reform. Its influence can be traced in the work of Charles Booth, and through him to the Chicago school of urban sociology in the twentieth century.[3]

For a larger, long-term relevance however, *Town Swamps* can, if coupled with Godwin's other extensive work as editor of *The Builder* for almost forty years, be considered in a third related framework: for the contribution which it makes towards a more informed understanding of urbanization as a global process and, ancillary to this, towards the development of a more comprehensive, comparative urban theory. Such a theory might assist in the assimilation and ordering of social and historical data if not in their interpretation.[4] This framework is appropriate for Godwin himself, one of the earliest supporters of the National Association for the Promotion of Social Science[5] and a committed proponent of the need for systematic social analysis.

II

The greater part of *Town Swamps and Social Bridges* had originally appeared in *The Builder*, the foremost architectural and building periodical in England for much of the nineteenth century. The distribution of the journal being far greater than that of the book, a proper assessment of the contents of *Town Swamps* must necessarily consider their original place of publication, and take account of the role of Godwin and *The Builder* in the context of social change in nineteenth-century England.

It is now evident that the rapid acceleration in what was to become a global process of urbanization began at the turn of the eighteenth to the nineteenth century.[6] In an increasingly industrial England, the greatest intercensal population increase which the country has ever recorded, either before or since, took place in the decade in which Godwin was born (1811–21). Vast numbers of this population were to become first-generation urban dwellers, many of them having to make the social, economic and psychological adjustments which the rural–urban transition demands. During Godwin's lifetime (1813–88) the percentage of the country's inhabitants living in towns in England and Wales grew from approximately 20 to 70; between 1831 and 1841, the decade in which he began his professional life, the population of some of the largest industrial cities such as Manchester, Liverpool and Leeds experienced an unprecedented growth of well over 40 per cent.[7]

Related to this unparalleled urban expansion, significant developments were taking place in the communications system, not only in transport but also in the production and distribution of print. Between 1840 and the end of the century, the basis of a mass readership market, the first of its kind in history, was being created. Three factors were responsible for this. Technical innovations revolutionized the speed of printing, raising output from 10,000 to 200,000 imprints per hour. Between 1855 and 1861 the so-called 'taxes on knowledge' were removed,[8] paving the way for a genuine mass media. Increasing literacy both resulted from and contributed to these developments. In the rapidly growing cities, the greater specialization which urbanization brings was reflected in the growth of increasingly specialized journals, each creating and holding its own readership.[9]

These developments, economic, social, and technical, led to other changes in the structure of society. Industrialization, with its continuing application of technology, meant greater specialization. New occupational roles were created and social differentiation increased. Not only did the number of artisans and mechanics grow; the proportion of full-time intellectual roles increased.[10] One of these new roles was that of the architectural journalist.

In the late eighteenth century, architectural writing was a minor pursuit, patronized by a small aristocratic elite. Though architectural and building monographs were produced, there is nothing which can be described as a regular, professional publication in this field.

By the early nineteenth century, these conditions had changed. The building trade had expanded sufficiently, both in manpower and money, to support its own specialized press. Significantly, the first number of *The Builder* was aimed at the 150,000 "carpenters and other building artificers", as well as architects, surveyors and others in the building profession. During the course of the nineteenth century, the building industry, most immediately responsible for shaping the urban environment, was to become the second largest in the country.[11] Secondly, technical innovations in printing had made possible a new type of literature, "the modern magazine, lavishly illustrated, inexpensive, and published at regular, frequent intervals".[12] The stage was set for the emergence of the architectural journalist.

The first identifiable occupant of this role was J. C. Loudon, described at his death in 1844 as "the originator of architectural journalism in this country".[13] By then, a substantial professional, middle-class and commercial readership existed for a periodical press centred on the building industry. The pioneer in this area, *The Architectural Magazine*, begun in 1834 and edited by Loudon, collapsed in 1838. *The Civil Engineer and Architectural Journal* was more specifically technical than general. Another journal, *The Surveyor, Engineer and Architect*, lasted only three years (1840–3).[14]

It was left for *The Builder*, founded in 1842 by J. A. Hansom (remembered more for his cab than his journalism), but after 1844 edited by Godwin, to capture this new and expanding market. For a journal with leanings towards urban reform the time was ideal. Chadwick's *Report on the Sanitary Condition of the Labouring Population* had appeared in 1842; the Royal Commission on the State of Large Towns and Populous Districts reported in 1844. From the 1840s on, the volume of criticism directed at conditions in the historically unique phenomenon of the industrial town increased.[15]

Immediately Godwin took over he expanded the coverage. For a decade before the repeal of the Stamp Tax, the paper had a virtual monopoly in its chosen fields. Of its subsequent competitors, *Building News* began only in 1855, *The Architect* in 1869 and the *British Architect* in 1874. *The Builder*, through its advertisements as well as its wide coverage, maintained a large clientele throughout the period, not least among the influential elite of Victorian Britain. Read by Samuel Smiles, contributed to be leading engineers, architects and builders, it was described by Florence Nightingale as "that excellent paper, *The Builder*". Its pages are said to have inspired Prince Albert's interest in the movement for sanitary reform.[16]

III

A major influence for improvement in the quality of nineteenth-century English urban life is the gradual change in values, attitudes and assumptions of the urban inhabitant towards his environment which took place throughout the century. Though explanations vary regarding the mechanisms by which these changes took place, factors such as awareness, motivation, persuasion, education and the influence of major reference groups are some of the important variables which must be considered.

As the contents of *Town Swamps* illustrate, much of Godwin's journalism was devoted to establishing such an awareness, to persuading, educating, and disseminating information. "The first step towards obtaining a remedy", he writes, "is to make the existence of the disease known" (page 12). His comments were not merely generalized complaints about slums: he personally inspected the grimmest of areas and then named them. On other occasions, unique among his contemporaries, he painstakingly traced the shifts in residence of families driven from slum to slum by railway developments. The assumption that certain areas were what his contemporaries termed as 'nuisance neighbourhoods', to be polluted at will by noxious industries, had to be questioned. Prejudices about living in flats had to be overcome (pages 65–6). One of the best ways of effecting changes in attitude was by education, and the earlier, the better: "the infant school is the lever by which the improvement of society must be worked". Public opinion regarding "sanitary and social reform" had to change. As the mediators of change Godwin identified "societies, individuals and leading workmen", particularly individuals in elite positions "like clergymen and surgeons who . . . not only do good in the practice of their vocations but also spread knowledge of matters which require change" (pages 29–30).

What insights can be gained from *Town Swamps and Social Bridges* into the system of social relations in Victorian Britain, into the nature of authority in society and the social and political philosophy of a representative middle-class Victorian mind? How does Godwin perceive his own civic role as well as the roles of others on whose behalf he writes?

Though some "wretched members of society" had fallen on bad times, we were yet "brothers and sisters of one great family", a family where more fortunate, "skilful and powerful men" had obligations, and property had "its duties as well as its rights", an axiom that had been left out of sight at the present time. There were two motives for exercising these duties, "pure high-souled unselfishness" that "happily is not rare among us" and "the commercial spirit, which is ready at all times to undertake whatever is likely to afford a good return for the money invested". In *Town Swamps*, the latter was more strongly present in Godwin's thought than it was twenty years later; in re-housing the urban poor "capitalists were watching the experiment" and "money will not be wanting to rear any description of dwellings which will return a fair profit on the outlay".

The "high-souled unselfishness" was rooted in a system of religious belief which was assumed rather than explicitly stated. Society was founded on a system of trusteeship with the accepted stewards of earthly wealth responsible for the welfare of their less privileged brethren; it was a society composed of "various classes" with the "need of sympathy" to bind them close together.

Physical and moral deterioration was caused directly by the environment, a philosophy aptly summed up in Godwin's maxim, "As the Homes, so the People". The main causes of urban crime and shortened lives were threefold: "ill-arranged dwellings, want of proper education" and the "lack of honest employment for the children". If homes were improved and children educated the numbers of " 'the dangerous classes' " would be lessened, suffering and misery would be prevented, lives extended, and "the sum of general wealth and general happiness" increased in true Utilitarian fashion; another solution for "taming the radicalism of the working class"[17] was to transport it to the suburbs. For those who have the inclination but not the opportunity to work, more chances of employment should be created; but for those youths

accustomed to irregular habits, the most hopeful way is to remove them from the scenes to which they have been accustomed, and where they are beset with temptations on all sides. The sea, our infant colonies, and the army, are means that might be made much more available than at present for the purpose of placing numbers who would be otherwise lost to society in comparative comfort.

In 1859, Godwin, like his contemporary Samuel Smiles, saw perseverance and self-reliance as the two cardinal virtues. Middle- and upper-class elites owed a moral duty to their fellow human beings to encourage them to help themselves; this they might do through the principle of co-operation, whether for housing provision, education, medical attention or to get themselves buried.

Where Godwin does go somewhat beyond his contemporaries is in his progressive views on education, an interest pursued through the pages of *The Builder* and embracing fields as wide apart as kindergartens and architectural education. Views on the education of infants and women are expressed briefly in *Town Swamps*; there are also references to his continuing concern for visual education (pages 18 and 45). His comments on the role of toys ("toys ought to be made to advance education") are typical of his interest in the work of Pestalozzi and Froebel. His views on art and its function as an agency of moral improvement, mentioned only in passing here, are discussed at length elsewhere.[18]

What, in terms of this philosophy and of the solutions proferred in *Town Swamps*, are Godwin's strategies for effecting change? Though three are mentioned, legislation, voluntarism, and "the commercial spirit", it is the last two which, in the late 1850s, he sees to be the most relevant. In this, Godwin is largely at one with his contemporaries; though sensitive to the inadequacies of the economic and political system, he is not willing, at least at this stage, to question its basic premises. Only in later life does he acknowledge that free-enterprise capitalism is inadequate to deal, without government intervention, with the problems which it itself creates. For the generation of the 'fifties it was still possible to assume a society based on rights and duties; if sufficient publicity was given to the rents in the social fabric, voluntary action, the chance to make a profit, and an unrepresentative legislature would hasten to the rescue.[19]

Basically, Godwin's "town swamps" represented the actual breakdowns in social organization as well as what he considers to be their cause; his swamps are not only crime, poverty, disease, sickness, unemployment and economic distress but also ignorance, superstition, overcrowding, pollution, the lack of recreational and educational provision, bad drainage, noxious industries and "that fateful swamp", drink. His system of "bridges" amounts to the voluntary establishment of virtually the whole of the institutional infrastructure required by an urban society; various levels of educational provision, ragged schools, complete with dormitories and industrial training, infant nurseries, vocational training schools, particularly for women, mechanics' institutes, juvenile reformatories, hospitals and dispensaries, homes for working girls, public playgrounds and recreational facilities, low-cost housing, services such as clothing clubs, social insurance schemes, organizations for social action (such as the *Society for Improving the Conditions of the Labouring Classes*), savings banks and homes for the destitute. More abstract "bridges" were conceived in terms of the need for behavioural change, such as the more frequent mixing together of representatives of different social classes, and the promotion of art as a means of social and moral development.

IV

Godwin was born in 1813, the son of a Kensington architect. Raised in the craft-oriented tradition of architectural apprentice-ship, his interests and talents were many. His formidable energy enabled him to accomplish much even before he became *The Builder's* editor at the age of thirty. Like the journal itself, Godwin's mind respected no intellectual compartments. By the age of twenty-three he had received the first Silver Medal ever awarded by the Institute of British Architects for a technical paper on the properties and applications of concrete, a paper which remained a standard work on the subject throughout the century. A second medal was received from the Société Libre des Beaux Arts in Paris for work in architectural history. Some-what later, he became one of the youngest men to be made a Fellow of the Royal Society; a contemporary journal describes him as "one of our younger architects whose energy and industry must give a new impetus to the art". Before taking over *The Builder*, Godwin had travelled widely in Europe, making the kind of 'grand tour' appropriate to an architect's education in his own day. His concern for social conditions had been expressed, not only in a paper on 'Architecture for the Poor', but also as member of a group which had lobbied the Prime Minister for metropolitan improvements, all this some years before the appearance of Chadwick's *Report on the Sanitary Condition of the Labouring Population* in 1842.

In addition, Godwin had lectured and written on church design, architectural history, aesthetics, the conservation and restoration of historic buildings, and had actively participated in adult education. In 1840, one of his numerous though mainly unpublished plays had been produced on the London stage. Most important of all, in active co-operation with Edward Edwards, Godwin had been instrumental in founding what was to become the most successful and popular organization for the promotion of art in Victorian England, the Art Union of London. The Union had two major functions: to diffuse to the public aesthetic principles and the moral values they were thought to incorporate, and to provide a system of patronage for an expanding profession of artists. The history of this organization represents an interesting case-study in the changing relationship between the artist and his public during the emergence of a modern industrial state. In the mainly agrarian, though industrializing society of the eighteenth century, patronage of the arts had come largely from an aristocratic and merchant elite. During the nineteenth century, this patronage was increasingly dependent on an expanding commerce- and industry-supported middle class. The role which the Art Union of London played in this transformation, and the repercussions which this transition had on the content, form, techniques and financing of art is told elsewhere.[20]

In recognition of these and many other activities, in 1881 Godwin was awarded the R.I.B.A. Gold Medal, an honour shared with Charles Barry, Lloyd Wright and, in our own day, Le Corbusier.

The strengths and weaknesses of Godwin's scientific orientation, in many ways representative of his contemporaries, are well illustrated in *Town Swamps and Social Bridges*. Chapter xvi on "Superstition and Belief" comprises an interesting if self-conscious vignette in which Godwin applies some basic principles of science to superstitions surrounding the phenomenon of death, an amateur's exploratory investigations into the history of science. As an investigator, his methods and standards of social inquiry varied: on occasion, as with his appreciation of the culturally determined behaviour of the Jews and their ritual practices at the time of death (page 31) he could be immensely perceptive; likewise, the description of Petticoat Lane (pages 32–5) would do justice to any aspiring social anthropologist. His ability to interpret quantitative data is less sophisticated, though it is perhaps unsympathetic to criticize Godwin's neglect of relevant variables such as occupation, age or nutritional level in his crude comparison of the death rates of Eastbourne (1·5 per cent) and Southwark (3·3 per cent), about which he is so incensed (page 68). Nor can we expect Godwin to have, in 1859, a more informed understanding of the bacteriological origin of disease. Of the three basic theories of disease prevalent in the mid-nineteenth century, Godwin, like many of his lay contemporaries, supported what was variously referred to as the 'atmospheric', 'miasmic', 'aerial' or 'pythogenic' theory.[21] This explains his obsession with light, air, and ventilation, expressed in the vocabulary of 'sanitary science', with its fear of 'deadly emanations', 'foul gases', 'foetid and pestiferous exhalations', and the 'vitiated atmosphere'.

Godwin's contacts were many. Apart from his R.I.B.A. membership he was in close touch with professional bodies such as the Institute of Civil Engineers, the Institute of Builders and many others. He maintained close liaison with such interest groups as the Metropolitan Improvement Society, the Health of Towns Association, the Saturday Half Holiday Association, the Society for Free Admission to National Monuments and others, all founded to mobilize public opinion in favour of their objectives. Godwin's contacts with them and the coverage he gave to their activities in *The Builder*, contributed significantly towards the diffusion of their ideas. His lifelong residence in South Kensington, a residential district much favoured by the middle- and upper-class elite of Victorian London, no doubt extended his personal network. It was probably with these influences in mind that a writer described *The Builder* in 1872 as "one of the finest properties in the categories of the weekly Press . . . its circulation is large . . . it enjoys among engineers, architects, builders and the members of other kindred professions and trades a reputation of the highest kind".[22] In this light, the encomiums bestowed by eminent and highly respected architects at Godwin's death would seem deserved. According to Alfred Waterhouse, at the height of his career the most eminent architect in the country, "probably the cause of sanitary science owes more to him than to any other man".[23] For Robert Kerr, Professor of the Arts of Construction at King's College, London, Godwin had been "a man behind the scenes in all artistic matters, a leader in many important movements which lay under the surface of affairs, and did not come prominently before the public".[24]

In retrospect, it is now clear that *The Builder* performed an indispensable function as a medium of communication for all those concerned with the urban process. Who these groups were was not immediately obvious in 1844. There is no better proof of this than to trace the evolution of its sub-title. In the early years, Godwin could only guess *where* a readership might be; when he retired, in 1883, it was directed specifically to those professions most immediately responsible for shaping the urban environment.[25]

V

If the role of Godwin and *The Builder* in improving the quality of urban life is to be adequately appreciated, attention needs to be given to another facet of his work of which there is some evidence in *Town Swamps*. This is his contribution to the accelerated application, organization and institutionalization of science and technology which took place throughout the century.[26]

An important element in this process was the professionaliza-
tion of occupations, including those of architecture and the various
branches of engineering. The creation of professional associations
with established criteria for recruitment, shared norms of
professional behaviour and a distinctive ethic governing members'
conduct was a major factor in the development of Victorian
technology. Purpose-built premises, specialized libraries and the
institution of regular meetings made possible a more adequate
exchange of ideas and information, an indispensable part of
scientific activity. One outcome of such meetings was the founding
of professional journals, significant for the wider circulation of
ideas. It is clear that these organizational changes, dependent as
they were on technical improvements in the communication and
distribution system, immensely increased the rate at which the
corpus of any particular knowledge grew, whether in medicine,
science, politics or the arts. The exponential growth of science, a
phenomenon so well recognized in the mid-twentieth century,[27]
owes much to the organizational and institutional infrastructure
laid in the nineteenth.

It is of some significance therefore, that of all the professional
or qualifying associations formed in Britain before 1888 (when
Godwin died), 76 per cent had been established during his own
lifetime (1813–1888).[28] Godwin was one of the first members of
one of the earliest of these, the Institute of British Architects,
founded in 1834 and becoming "Royal" in 1837. Amongst its
strongest supporters, he provided in *The Builder* a vehicle in
which most of the social, technical and aesthetic issues of the day
were thrashed out by the professional people responsible for them.
A glance at its pages will show the very significant role it played
in the institutionalization of norms appropriate, not only to the
new profession of architect, but also to the idea of professionalism
itself. "He took a very deep interest in the affairs of the Institute,
and, for forty years, he pulled the strings (so to speak), in favour
of it, as no one else could have done."[29]

The Builder's function was manifold; it provided a reporting
service by which professional knowledge stemming from meetings

of doctors, builders, engineers, architects and others was distributed at a national level; it provided an abstracting service by which the gist of technical papers was made available both to the industry and to the lay public; it printed news of the meetings of pressure groups devoted to improving the quality of the urban environment; it acted as a sounding board for the discussion of technical opinion; by its advertisements as much as its coverage it functioned as a leading instrument in the diffusion of scientific and technical know-how.

Godwin was both an innovator and a diffuser of innovation. For many years he had advocated what would now be called system-building, the mass production of doors, windows and other building units, as a means of reducing the cost of working-class accommodation.[30] As the principal building expert on the Royal Commission on the Housing of the Working Classes, 1884–5, he made one of his last public contributions to urban reform by drawing attention to experiments in system-built concrete construction. Ever since his prize-winning essay of 1836, he had been one of the major advocates of concrete as a building material; "it is largely due to his enthusiasm that so much acrimonious polemic on the subject was thrashed out in detail in the pages of his weekly review".[31]

On the same occasion, Godwin drew attention to another innovation which he had frequently advocated: high-rise blocks of flats. This idea, originally developed in France, he first publicized in *The Builder* and subsequently at the Social Science Congress of 1865. A stage in the development of this viewpoint, and some reference to public attitudes towards it, are mentioned briefly in *Town Swamps* (pages 65–6, 85).

Similar concern for innovation can be seen in Godwin's interest in ventilation engineering, and in his support for Florence Nightingale's campaign to promote revolutionary changes in the design and planning of hospitals (pages 70–3). Broadly speaking, these developments transformed British hospitals from the multi-storeyed and hotel-like blocks of the eighteenth century to a series of single-storeyed and separated pavilions, each linked together by long and often open corridors. Though they were based on a mistaken 'aerial' theory of disease which, simply stated, taught that infection was conveyed by polluted air, the debate which the controversy generated helped to provide Britain with more hospitals than at any time in her previous history. The episode, and the *Builder's* place in it, was instrumental in bringing about a total change in the planning and building of hospitals for the remainder of the century.[32]

VI

Though the conditions described by Godwin in *Town Swamps* are widely separated both in time and space from those now being experienced in urban regions in other parts of the world, the similarity between them is too great to resist making comparisons whilst still acknowledging differences. One can pick at random any one of the many studies of urbanization in the so-called 'developing countries'; typical is a relatively recent account of the fringe slums of Santiago with its list of urban ills representative of conditions in many comparable cities in the ex-colonial world: lack of running water, sewage systems unknown, water available only infrequently and then at high cost, no garbage collection, schools and hospitals non-existent or inaccessible, self-built settlements far from the centre of towns and, therefore, from employment opportunities, transport costly in time and money, the settlement "often built on the garbage dump itself" (see *Town Swamps*, p. 23) and, the worst aspect of all, insecurity of tenancy with the possibility of being thrown out at a moment's notice.[33]

All these phenomena can be recognized in Godwin's writing, though only some are represented in this particular volume. Here, in addition to what he very graphically describes as "town swamps", are other attributes of the rapidly industrializing, expanding city: the persistence in the town of rural patterns of behaviour; the heterogenous growth of neighbourhoods and their pollution by uncontrolled small-scale industry; the effect of changing property values on the residential patterns of the poor;

the problem of urban employment posed by technological obsolescence; the lack of provision for the myriad of social, economic and political needs generated by the social and technical dimensions of urbanization.

There is neither sufficient material in *Town Swamps and Social Bridges* alone nor sufficient space in this introduction to pursue the fundamental question which data of this kind suggest, namely, what is universal about urbanization and what is not? More specifically, "in what degrees and in what respects is the social impact of urbanization modified by distinct cultural and historical traditions? Clearly, no two urbanizing societies experience identical transformations. But it is equally clear that there are similarities in the process through which two societies pass."[34] Familiarity with all of Godwin's work, and with the mass of evidence and comment on the urbanization process in England, coupled with an awareness of contemporary material on the same phenomena would help us analyse these comparative issues with more confidence.

If historians and social scientists are prepared to make full use of the secondary authorities available,[35] perhaps a more comprehensive body of comparative urban theory can be built up from the immense amount of data accumulated from cities all over the world. It is only within such a comparative framework that the study of an individual city can be understood.[36] In contributing towards the development of such a theory, and at the same time, enabling us to identify more clearly the distinct social and cultural characteristics peculiar to urbanization and other aspects of change in nineteenth-century British society, *Town Swamps and Social Bridges* has a valuable contribution to make.

Anthony D. King
Leicester, March 1971

NOTES

1. See Ruth Glass, 'Urban Sociology in Great Britain: A Trend Report', *Current Sociology*, IV (1955), p. 8.
2. See the introduction by Anthony S. Wohl to Andrew Mearns' *The Bitter Cry of Outcast London* (1883: Victorian Library, Leicester University Press, 1970) including the detailed notes. A comprehensive historical account of nineteenth-century slums is given in H. J. Dyos, 'The Slums of Victorian London', *Victorian Studies*, XI, no. 1 (September 1967).
3. Glass, *op. cit.* See also E. Shils, 'The History of Sociology', *Daedalus*, vol. 99, no. 4 (Fall 1970), pp. 760–825.
4. For a well-documented statement on this viewpoint see G. S. Sjoberg, 'Comparative Urban Sociology' in R. K. Merton, L. Broom, L. S. Cottrell, Jr., *Sociology Today* (New York, 1959) especially p. 359. Also Val R. Lorwin, 'Historians and other social scientists: the comparative analysis of nation-building in Western societies' and Reinhard Bendix, 'Concepts in comparative historical analysis' in Stein Rokkan (ed.), *Comparative Research across Cultures and Nations* (Paris, 1968).
5. Founded in 1856.
6. See Eric E. Lampard, 'Historical Aspects of Urbanization' in P. M. Hauser and L. F. Schnore, *The Study of Urbanization* (New York, 1965), p. 522.
7. W. Ashworth, *The Genesis of Modern British Town Planning* (1954), pp. 8–9.
8. The government abolished advertising duties in 1853, stamp duty in 1855 and the taxes on paper in 1861.
9. J. W. Saunders, *The Profession of English Letters* (1964), p. 201. I am indebted to Professor P. A. W. Collins for this reference.
   Saunders shows that the number of periodicals and newspapers in England increased from 563 in 1851 to just over 2000 in 1870. By 1900 there were 4934, half of which were periodicals.
10. See Bernard Barber, 'The Sociology of Science', contribution under 'Science' to the *International Encyclopaedia of Social Sciences* (New York, 1968), vol. 14, p. 96.
11. The building and construction industry is taken here to include the allied industries of bricks, cement, glass, pottery, wood,

furniture, fittings and decoration, whose interests *The Builder* covered. B. Mitchell and P. Deane, *Abstract of British Historical Statistics* (1962), chapter II.

12. Frank Jenkins, 'Nineteenth Century Architectural Periodicals' in J. Summerson (ed.), *Concerning Architecture: Essays on Architectural Writing presented to Nikolaus Pevsner* (1968), p. 153. I am indebted to Alan Crawford for this reference.

13. *Art Union Journal*, January 1844.

14. Jenkins, *op. cit.*, p. 154.

15. Dyos, *op. cit.*, pp. 11–12. It should not be assumed, however, that the peculiarly English concern with urban sanitation and drainage was a uniquely Victorian phenomenon. Apart from other eighteenth-century cases in England, one might quote the report of the East India Company's surveyor on the drains and sewage system of Benares, written in 1790. See B. S. Cohn, 'The British in Benares: A 19th Century Colonial Society', *Comparative Studies in Society and History*, IV (1961–2), pp. 169–208.

16. *The Times*, 30 January 1888.

17. Glass, *op. cit.*, p. 3.

18. Anthony King, 'George Godwin and the Art Union of London, 1837–1911', *Victorian Studies*, VIII, no. 2 (December 1964), pp. 101–130.

19. It is interesting to compare Godwin's views as presented in *Town Swamps* with the comprehensive framework provided by Reinhard Bendix, *Nation-Building and Citizenship* (New York, 1964), particularly the section on Transformations of Western European Societies, pp. 39–89, (Anchor Edition, 1969).

20. See note 18 above.

21. The three were the germ theory, the theory of 'spontaneous generation', and the 'atmospheric' theory which held that "under certain mysterious circumstances . . . the atmosphere became charged with an 'epidemic influence' which in turn became malignant when it combined with the exhalations of organic decompositions from the earth. The resultant gases, ferments or miasms (the agents were diverse) produced diseases." It was a theory which "concentrated attention on environmental problems rather than those of personal health and infection". Royston Lambert, *Sir John Simon, 1816–1904, and English Social Administration* (1963), p. 49. Lambert gives a detailed and

excellent account of these theories (pp. 49–55) and the entire public health movement.

22. J. Grant, *History of the Newspaper Press* (1872), p. 122.

23. R.I.B.A. *Proceedings*, vol. 4, N.S. (9 February 1888). Waterhouse was President of the R.I.B.A. 1888–91. He had been honoured by awards from Austria, Holland, Belgium, Italy, France and Germany.

24. *Ibid.*, p. 143.

25. From being "an illustrated weekly for the drawing room, studio, office and workshop" in 1844, with somewhat parochial aspirations, by 1883 it had become a journal "for the Architect, Engineer, Archaeologist, Constructor, Sanitary Reformer and Art-Lover".

26. The processes involved in the organization and institutionalization of science in the nineteenth century are not particularly well documented. Exceptions are Joseph Ben-David, 'Scientific Productivity and Academic Organization in Nineteenth Century Medicine', *American Sociological Review*, vol. 25 (1960), pp. 828–843. A recent study is that by B. W. G. Holt, 'Social aspects in the emergence of chemistry as an exact science: the British chemical profession', *British Journal of Sociology*, vol. XXI (2 June 1970). See also the introduction by G. Basalla, W. Coleman and R. H. Kargon to *Victorian Science* (New York, 1970).

27. See for example, Derek de la Solla Price, *Little Science, Big Science* (New York, 1963).

28. G. Millerson, *The Qualifying Associations* (1964). Chronological List of Existing Qualifying Associations, Appendix II, p. 246.

Among those most immediately connected with the construction of the Victorian city can be mentioned the Institutes of Civil Engineers (1818), Builders (1834), British Architects (1834), Mechanical Engineers (1847), Surveyors (1868), the Architectural Association (1847), Civil and Mechanical Engineering Society (1859), British Association of Gas Surveyors (1873) and the Society of Telegraph Engineers (1887).

As Carr-Saunders points out, the number of professions increased with the number of new techniques (A. M. Carr-Saunders and R. A. Wilson, *The Professions* (1933), p. 158). This is most effectively indicated by the increasing specialization in engineering reflected in the founding of professional associations devoted to different branches of engineering: civil (1818), mechanical (1847), mining (1852), gas (1863), telegraph (1871) (to become the Institute of Electrical Engineers in 1888), municipal and sanitary (1873), marine (1889), sanitary (1895), water (1896), to name only those in the nineteenth century.

Barrington Kaye gives a list of professional associations all based on "the application of scientific techniques to industry". Barrington Kaye, *The Development of the Architectural Profession in Britain* (1960), p. 3.

29. Robert Kerr, Professor of the Arts of Construction, King's College, London: R.I.B.A. *Proceedings*, vol. 4, N.S. (9 February 1888), p. 143.

30. A more extensive discussion of Godwin's contribution to the introduction of system-building in England is given in Anthony King, 'Another Blow for Life: George Godwin and the Reform of Working Class Housing', *Architectural Review*, vol. 136, no. 814 (December 1964), pp. 448–52.

31. Peter Collins, *Concrete: The Vision of a New Architecture* (1959), p. 39.

32. For the part played by Godwin and *The Builder* in bringing about changes in the design and planning of hospitals, see Anthony King, 'Hospital Planning: Revised Thoughts on the Origin of the Pavilion Principle in England', *Medical History*, vol. X, no. 4 (October 1966), pp. 360–73.

33. Andrew G. Frank, 'Urban Poverty in Latin America', *Studies in Comparative International Development*, vol. II, no. 5 (1966), pp. 75–82.

34. David B. Carpenter, 'Urbanization in the United States and Japan', *Studies in Comparative International Development*, vol. II, no. 3 (1966), pp. 37–49. See also Rhoades Murphey, 'Historical and Comparative Urban Studies' in R. G. Putnam, F. J. Taylor, P. G. Kettle, *A Geography of Urban Places: Selected Readings* (Toronto, 1970), pp. 25–32. "With the creation of a global commercial network, the spread of industrialization and the technological revolution in transport and transferability, cities everywhere are becoming more like one another . . . confronting the same kind of problems." (p. 32).

35. Lorwin, *op. cit.*, p. 106.

36. Sjoberg, *op. cit.*

BIBLIOGRAPHICAL NOTE

Town Swamps and Social Bridges. The Sequel of "A Glance at the Homes of the Thousands", by George Godwin, was published in London by Routledge, Warnes, & Routledge in 1859. The present volume reprints photographically the whole of this text.

J. L. Madden

THE RISING GENERATION TAKING THEIR LESSONS.

A Penny Theatre in London.

TOWN SWAMPS

AND

SOCIAL BRIDGES.

THE SEQUEL OF

"A Glance at the Homes of the Thousands."

BY

GEORGE GODWIN, F.R.S.

EDITOR OF "THE BUILDER," ETC.

"Arise! for the day is passing,
While you lie dreaming on;
Your brothers are cased in armour,
And forth to the fight are gone.
Your place in the ranks awaits you,
Each man has a part to play;
The Past and the Future are nothing
In the face of the stern To-day."

With numerous Engravings done from the Life.

LONDON:
ROUTLEDGE, WARNES, & ROUTLEDGE,
FARRINGDON STREET.
1859.

LONDON :

COX AND WYMAN, PRINTERS, GREAT QUEEN STREET,

LINCOLN'S-INN FIELDS.

INTRODUCTORY.

I⊤ is interesting to know what is going on around us, how our neighbours live, and what are the circumstances in operation to shape their character, and lead to actions which will work on others, and may on ourselves. Nothing interests man like man : and this alone perhaps would afford sufficient reason for the publication of the following pages. Moreover, some may specially like to know of a few of the agencies that are in operation tending to lift the multitude out of the slough, and to learn in what way they could themselves help in bringing this about. Further, it might be urged, that this little volume will hereafter interest the inquirer and the antiquary, as a record of the curious—not to say frightful —condition of London and some of its denizens in the middle of the boasted nineteenth century. I avoid giving too serious a reason for producing it, lest it should repel ever so few readers. It has been done, however, in no trifling or book-making spirit, and it is offered with a strong feeling on the subject to the most serious consideration of the public. A fact may perhaps prove that its warnings ought not to be disregarded.

In the little work called "London Shadows—a Glance at the Homes of the Thousands," of which this is a Sequel, it was shown that thousands of our countrymen and countrywomen are condemned to exist in this metropolis in dens where cleanliness is impossible, and health and morals are alike speedily degraded ;

where children are educated downwards, and made criminals with little fault of their own ; and it was sought to evoke in their aid, not merely

" The pure high-soul'd unselfishness,"

that happily is not rare amongst us, but the commercial spirit, which is ready at all times to undertake whatever is likely to afford a good return for money invested.   The statements therein made, many months before the cholera descended on the metropolis, were justified in the most remarkable manner ; for it will surely be considered as something more than a coincidence when it is seen, that the first illustration in that work is taken from the neighbourhood of Berwick-street and Broad-street, Golden-square, where occurred that frightful visitation which carried nearly 700 persons to their graves in a few days ; while the concluding engraving represents the condition of the houses about Ewer-street and Gravel-lane, Southwark, where the disease gave the last serious manifestation of its power in the metropolis !   It is not presumption to assert that if the advice therein given had been attended to, thousands of lives might have been saved, and thousands of pounds.   It will be long before that frightful night and day, when the disease reigned in Broad-street and Berwick-street, are forgotten ; when men stood in groups, awe-struck and paralyzed, and Death hovered over every house, leaving desolate homes and fatherless children to mark his fearful track.   Enough, however, on this head.

The little volume in question enlisted the sympathies, of the periodical press in a remarkable manner, and led to many valuable articles and to expressions on the part of individuals, which might be usefully printed, if it could be done without fear of displeasing.   To take half a dozen from fifty :—the Prime Minister of the day, Lord Palmerston, acknowledged it as " an interesting volume;" Earl Stanhope, then Lord Mahon, thought it "a very curious Essay on a very important, though hitherto neglected subject;" Lord Shaftesbury said, "The horrible truths of your book ought to stir us all to exertion, but my own wearisome experience of many years leads me to think that we shall do very little;" Lord Londesborough wrote, "Alas! it is a true and perfectly faithful picture,—but even in the country, where the painful *squalor* of poverty does not exist, I find in the habitations of the labourers a want of thought on the part of the builders, producing a crop of vice and crime of a hideous nature, that might be remedied at the slightest imaginable cost;" Lord Ebrington said, "I am able to corroborate from personal inspection some few, and from official knowledge most, of the reports and descriptions. May your words, and the too faithful horrors of the illustrations, help to arouse the public from that foolish and wicked apathy with which sanitary reform has been for some time viewed, to a proper sense of its interests and its duties in relation to the prevalence and continuance of a state of things not less expensive to us if economically, than dangerous to us if politically and socially considered,—not less discreditable to us as a civilized, than sinful in us as a Christian community;" Mr. John Walter, M.P. wrote,— "The subject of your very interesting work is one of which it is impossible to overrate the magnitude and importance;" Dr. Bickersteth expressed "the deep interest" with which he had read the statements, and the then Chief Commissioner of Her Majesty's Works, Sir Benjamin Hall, quoted them in the House of Commons, in support of his views when bringing in the Local Management Act for the Metropolis.

Something has been done since then, but comparatively little; and it is, partly, to remove the impression that further efforts are unnecessary, that this volume is issued.   Although some of the statements it contains appeared at an earlier date than this in the *Builder*, fresh examinations have been made, and the book must be taken as correctly representing the condition of things at the present time.

I would add, that throughout the lengthened and minute inquiry —of which this and the preceding little book give, after all, but a very limited view,—I have been materially assisted by Mr. John Brown, and am anxious to acknowledge the value of his services.

G. G.

BROMPTON,
February, 1859.

TOWN SWAMPS AND SOCIAL BRIDGES.

CHAPTER I.

THERE are dark and dangerous places—swamps and pitfalls—in the social world which need bridging over, to afford a way out to the miserable dwellers amidst degradation and filth. "God's blessing," writes Longfellow,—

> " God's blessing on the architects who build
> The bridges o'er swift rivers and abysses
> Before impassable to human feet,
> No less than on the builders of cathedrals,
> Whose massive walls are bridges thrown across
> The dark and terrible abyss of Death."

And blessings on those who build and maintain bridges over the swamps of great towns, otherwise impassable to thousands, and afford a chance of light and hope to poor souls born in darkness and misery.

After the writer had laid bare, systematically and constantly, for years, the frightful condition of various parts of this proud, populous, wealthy, overgrown London, the home of nearly three millions of people, the resort of the intellect of the world,—had shown the depths of the shadows lying here, there, and everywhere, at the back of the bright thoroughfares where fashion disports itself, the festers and malignant sores with which the body of society is spotted, though they are carefully hidden away,—it was said that enough had been told, that it was unnecessary to make the evil further known, and that improvement would surely follow. Improvement is not so easily obtained when the evil is of monster size : it takes a long time to make the public appreciate the necessity of it, and they must be told a thing many times before they will even hear, still oftener before they will move. Something has been done, and the life of man has been lengthened.

Nevertheless, the causes of premature and unnecessary deaths are still at work,—the hotbeds, growing a criminal population, are still allowed to remain. The City officer of health suddenly re-describes the unhealthy dens crowded with degraded life, pointed out by us years ago, and all London is perfectly astonished, its daily press in particular, that such a state of things could possibly exist. Eloquent leaders are written on all sides, some speeches perhaps made, and then all the facts are utterly forgotten, and the evil goes quietly on, doing its deadly work, and will be rediscovered by-and-by, again to be consigned to a convenient oblivion.

Quite recently the leading journal has described not merely similar unhealthy dens and their occupants, but literally the very same (Rose-alley, near Field-lane, Holborn, for example), showing the existence of the same frightful state of things at the present time ! The articles in question stirred London, and produced in reply an extraordinary subscription in aid of those who are in want,—not less than £13,000. Admirable was the intention ; noble has been the response. All honour be to those concerned :—

> " Not the king's crown, nor the deputed sword,
> The marshal's truncheon, nor the judge's robe,
> Become them with one half so good a grace
> As mercy does."

From the cradle to the grave, mankind need the aid of their fellows : we cannot exist without it,—high or low, rich or poor. It is a condition of our being : all who need aid have a right to ask it : none who are able to give it can refuse without danger.

Pecuniary aid, however, for those who were spoken of was not our object, as the readers of "London Shadows" know. What we had in view was to point out the causes which transform the poor to criminals, which sap alike their morals and their strength ; to induce the adoption of sanitary improvements ; and to bring to light some of the causes of evil largely in operation. It is to be hoped that they who have been moved to afford immediate aid to the necessitous, may be led to examine into these causes, and aid in removing them.

Something has been done in one direction, it is true, but to so small an extent that the body of the evil remains untouched : in parts, indeed, it is increased — the overcrowding is greater than ever. New streets are made without the slightest provision for the poor people who are turned out ; and they are forced to quarter themselves where there is no room for healthful existence. The question, where are they to go, never troubles the improver. In one of Mr. Planché's far-seeing extravaganzas, "The Birds of Aristophanes," the king of the birds says to one of the characters, who has induced him to build a city in the air for the birds,—

> " *King.* Where's Jackanoxides ? I come to tell,
> The city 's built—
> *Jack.*   'Tis well !
> *King.* I would 'twere well—
> *Jack.* Is't not well built ?
> *King.*   Yes.
> *Jack.* Well, then, what's the matter ?
> *King.* The rooks are making a confounded clatter ;
> They want a rookery—

> *Jack.*   In my new town!
>   By Jove, if they build one, I'll pull it down.
> *King.*   *They can't afford to live in Peacock-square ;*
>   Where can they go to ?
> *Jack.*   Go to ?—anywhere ! "

And so our new street-makers, when they are asked where the displaced occupants of the garrets and cellars are to go, shout without thought,—

> " Go to ?—anywhere ! "

Let them be wise in time, or it may lead to mischief greater than is dreamt of. Not long ago, Paris was in greater danger of a revolution through the destruction of the dwellings of the poor without the provision of other places of reception, than it had been for some time ; and the Comte de Tourdonnet, in the " *Revue Contemporaine*," warned proprietors to hear the voice of reason in time, and lower their demands ; since, however strong a government should be, it might yet be taken by surprise in the case of a sudden and universal outburst, and might be unable, at least for a time, to avert the vengeance of an infuriated multitude, of which the landlords would be the first victims.

Healthful dwellings, where the decencies of life may be maintained, juvenile reformatories, ragged schools, infant nurseries, and similar institutions, are then amongst our Social Bridges, and others will come into view as we proceed.

Foremost amongst the causes which lead to the increase of crime in London are,—Ignorance ; the want of the means for teaching children some useful trade ; and the neglect or ill-conduct of parents, who leave their offspring to shift for themselves, or drive them into the streets to thieve.

Take an illustration or two. A boy in the Reformatory in Britannia-street, Islington, said, when asked,—" I am between fourteen and fifteen years old. I have a father and stepmother, and two sisters younger than myself. I have been in prison three times. I stole once a loaf of bread : I was very hungry, and could get nothing to eat. I once stole some bacon, and took it home to divide with my sisters. My father, however, took up the poker and hit me with it, because I would not give him all."

The sufferings of this lad in the streets (for in course of time he was driven into them by his unnatural guardians) were too shocking to be related. The superintendent of the place said he did not know a letter in a book until he came there, and that he was then a good and industrious boy.

Some of the boys here go out in various ways to work, others are engaged chopping wood ; and out of ninety boys admitted since the opening of the school, sixty have been put in the way of earning their bread in an honest manner : several have entered the navy, others have become soldiers : some have been apprenticed to trades.

The boys, when first brought to these institutions, are in most instances ignorant of everything good. The superintendent of the Britannia-street Reformatory says—" Of the large number of boys who have passed through the school, very few have returned to their former habits." He knows many who, if they had been left in the street, would have been a pest to the country, but are now filling situations in life, and becoming useful members of society. The cost at which this amount of good is done seems very small :—little more than £6. 10s. per annum, or 2s. 6d. a week, for each lad. When we find criminals transported at a cost of from £30 to £40 a year each, one feels astonished that the various ragged schools and places of refuge are allowed to remain in struggling circumstances.

Questioning a group of lads of from twelve to sixteen years of age, at the Field-lane Ragged School, every one of them, without the least appearance of compunction, acknowledged that he had been either three, four, six, or seven times in prison. They had in most instances stolen food, and none of the half-dozen lads had either father or mother. Useful knowledge, when they first came to the school, they had none : how could they have it ? The report of the schools would afford dozens of instances of the mode in which children are forced to become thieves and vagabonds.

In the Field-lane school great good has been done by a society of ladies, who give clothing, and receive from the children part of the value of it in very small payments. The first properly-shaped articles of dress with which some of the children have been clothed have been obtained in this way.

Inquiry shows that there is a large class to deal with who are totally neglected, are without a shelter, and are obliged to break the law at a tender age in order to obtain the commonest necessaries of life. It is clearly proved that some of the wildest of them, if caught in time, can be transformed into useful members of society. It seems certain that ragged schools, in connection with dormitories and industrial training, if instituted to a sufficient extent in the proper neighbourhoods, will give a right impress instead of wrong, and effect much good. At any rate, it is but proper to try the effect of kindness and persuasion before taking other measures. It is an act of injustice to allow thousands of ignorant and destitute children, both male and female, to go to almost certain destruction, without an effort.

Let us look at the matter in a practical point of view. We want good artisans,—our colonies want them even more—offer money for them. Would it not be better, wiser, cheaper, for the country to turn the neglected infant population of our cellars and streets into men of this class, instead of allowing them to become, as they unquestionably must become if uncared for, rogues and thieves, if nothing worse, to plunder honester men, and to be ultimately caught, tried, convicted, and maintained in prison, or a penal settlement,—all at the cost of the State ?

CHAPTER II.

The condition of various parts of London, in a sanitary and social point of view, the improvements required, and the results of efforts now making with a view to amelioration, demand continuous attention. So many-sided is London, so numerous are the points of inquiry it presents, so enormous and weighty the interests involved, that it needs numerous endeavours before the whole can be grasped,— the co-operation of many minds before much can be effected. It is no easy task to get a clear idea, even, of this mighty maze,—

> " Of London, of its streets, its bridges, crowds ;
> St. Paul's, the broad moon sailing o'er the dome ;
> The rich-carved abbey, with its thousand frets
> And pinnacles, religious with the dead ;
> Of the brave spirits who go up to woo
> That terrible city whose neglect is death,
> Whose smile is fame ; the prosperous one who sits
> Sole in the summer sun ; the crowd who die
> Unmention'd, as a wave which forms and breaks
> On undiscover'd shores."*

It is necessary to make known to one half of its denizens how the other half live, and to this second half what the first half are doing for them. The readers of " London Shadows" know something of the abominations which are shrouded by the houses on the east side of *Gray's-inn-lane*, abominations of the most deadly kind. We spoke loudly enough about them when we began our inquiries into the condition of London dwelling-places, and laid bare a few of the plague-spots and fever-stills of the metropolis. Some may remember the account of Charlotte's-buildings there, and the view given of the front rooms of one house with its sixty inhabitants. Bell-court, Fox-court, Baldwin's-gardens, and Tyndall's-buildings, were pointed to ; and, remarking on how " few of the countless throngs who flood the paths in Gray's-inn-lane have any knowledge of the hotbeds of disease and vice which exist within a dozen yards of them," we called for the in-terference of some who had power or influence to cleanse and convert that fearful neighbourhood.

The title of the thoroughfare now filled, from early morning till late night, with the busiest of a busy community, speaks of the country. When we say " Gray's-inn-lane," there is a smell of new hay in the air, and we have a notion of singing-birds. In Van den Wyngrerde's View of London (1543), it is seen to be truly a lane leading from the Inn northwards to the retired village of St. Pan-cras, with only one building in the pleasant fields eastwards between

* Alexander Smith : "City Poems."

that and Ely House, where the strawberries grew. The Londoners found country air there, and men and maids went maying in the spring time. It was then called Purtpool or Portpool lane, from the manor of that name, through which it passed. It soon, however, took its present title, and in Stow's time was "furnished with fair buildings and many tenements on both the sides, leading to the fields towards Highgate and Hampstead."

The Inn-walks were much resorted to, and we may see with the mind's eye *Mr.* Francis Bacon superintending the "new rayle and quickset hedges" which were put up there under his direction. From this place (in 1597) he dated the first dedication to his "dear brother" of his wonderful Essays, which may be read and re-read throughout a life with pleasure and profit; and here, in the walks he had himself laid out, and the summer-house he had built, he pondered the new *Organum.* Later it was a fashionable resort; and we have Pepys, in 1662, "when church was done," walking "to Graye's Inne, to observe fashions of the ladies, because of" his "wife's making some clothes."

The degradation of the neighbourhood to its present condition is of much more recent date : to trace it is unnecessary : it has now reached its climax, and our appeal in favour of its miserable inhabitants has been heard and partially responded to.

Lord Shaftesbury's excellent "Society for Improving the Condition of the Labouring Classes" descended upon an utterly degraded part of it, *Tyndall's-buildings*, and has put it into a proper condition for occupation by human beings,—served it, in short, as it served Wild-court, Drury-lane, and we have no doubt with equally good results to the community,—preserving the capital of the poor man (his health), and presently, it is to be hoped, it will produce a good return for the capital of the society,—its money.

Tyndall's-buildings is a court containing twenty-two houses. Before the society had it, the shutters and doors were broken : from most of the windows projected a well-known apparatus for drying the day's "wash :" the pavement was broken and out of level, retaining decomposing matter to contaminate the air, while the basement story of nearly all the houses was filled with fœtid refuse, of which it had been the receptacle for years. In some of the houses it seemed scarcely possible that human beings could live : the floors were in holes, the stairs broken down, and the plastering had fallen ; nevertheless, they were densely peopled, and as much rent was paid for the rooms as ought to have obtained for the tenants decent accommodation. In one, the roof had fallen in : it was driven in by a tipsy woman one night, who sought to escape over the tiles from her husband. Listen to the conversation, if so it may be called, of those inhabiting it : you would find it in keeping with the disordered, disruptured, disreputable locality : notice the faces that press against the window-pane, or come out into the doorways as a stranger passes round the court : you would find them altogether in accordance,—as the house, so the inmate. Entering the doorway, we were shown a narrow staircase, dark as night, broken and shaky, down which we groped with bent back and much difficulty. At the bottom a glimmering light showed a water-barrel which would hold fifty ŏr sixty gallons at the most. It was at this time not eleven o'clock in the morning, and the water was all gone; and this was not to be wondered at, when we found that this barrel was the only supply furnished for two houses, which, at the lowest calculation, contained a population of one hundred persons, old and young—this to serve for all purposes of cleanliness and domestic use. In this dim undercroft was also the only convenience provided for the same number of persons :—that and the water in close proximity. The smell was abominable. The owners of such places say,—" People of this sort are naturally dirty, and it is useless to do anything with them." We would ask in reply,—" How is it possible that good habits can be acquired under such circumstances ?"

Since this visit, the place has been greatly altered and improved. A house at the bottom of the court has been cleared away to let in air ; the rooms and staircases have been plastered and whitewashed ; ventilation is provided for ; daylight let in where necessary ; and a proper supply of water provided : large rooms are divided by parti-tions, of such height as not to prevent the circulation of air, and yet afford decent sleeping accommodation for a family ; and the cellars have been cleaned. In other words, a set of dens and sties have been transformed into cleanly, orderly, and wholesome dwellings. The filthy state of the basements caused considerable delay in the opera-tions. The foul effluvia emitted actually rendered it impossible for the workmen to proceed for some time after the surface had been broken up, and many of them were taken ill.

Tyndall translated the Bible ; and the Society for Improving the Labouring Classes have obeyed its teaching in translating Tyndall's-buildings.

Charlotte's-buildings, close by, will afford a contrast. When we examined it a few days ago, it was, still, in an abominable condition. The atmosphere throughout the court was unbearable : the broken pavement was reeking with rotting matter : the houses are in ruins ; the inhabitants in misery. What the minds *must* be that are formed in such a mould, the world should by this time know.

In this and similarly neglected spots, a new generation is springing up, without care for education, decency, and in some instances, it is to be feared, honesty ; and nothing can be more disheartening than the aspect of the groups of lads, of from seven to eighteen years of age, visible in obscure corners, with sentinels posted to give notice of the approach of the police, busily engaged in gambling, and using language shocking to the ears. They have never had the chance of useful employment ; are learned in all mischief, but wanting in such knowledge as would fit them to be useful members of the community. It cannot be doubted that these dangerous weeds—which might have been useful plants—are increasing in an undue ratio, not only in London, but in other large towns.

No thinking person can glance without feelings of pity at the thousands who are thus thrown upon the world without a chance ; and many good men are endeavouring to find some remedy for the evil. Various plans have been suggested ; and great as may be the disputes on this subject, all will agree as to the impossibility of rearing useful men and women in such dens, and under such conditions as it has been our painful duty to describe.

In providing dwellings for the poorer classes in large towns, one of the chief things necessary is to get rid of the prejudices which exist, and make it difficult to persuade those who have been accustomed to certain dwellings to change them for others which are evidently better ; and in consequence, persons who own the inferior description of house property can point with a sort of triumph to the appreciation by their tenants, and the profits of their dwellings, in comparison with some of the model buildings which have been put up in London. We cannot, therefore, look without interest at the working of these institutions, feeling that those who have their management hold a great responsibility ; for capitalists are watching the experiment, and money will not be wanting to rear any description of dwellings which will return a fair profit upon the outlay.

The £. s. d. consideration is so important, that one or two circumstances in connection with the new buildings must be alluded to.

In the St. Pancras-road Building the sets of apartments consist of two and three rooms, and other accommodation : for these a rent is charged of 4s. 6d., 5s. 6d., 6s. 6d., and we believe some are priced as highly as 7s. a week (the latter amounting to £18. 4s. per annum), —a large sum when we consider that comfortable cottages can in many places be had for a trifle more ; and although the internal arrangements of these apartments are excellent, still it is evident that the rent here charged is more than can be afforded by the great body of mechanics, for whom this place was intended. Moreover, the style, approaches, and staircases, are not sufficiently attractive for those who can afford so much. Three or four years ago it was rare in this building to find any apartments to let. But the rents have been from time to time raised ; and since the last increase many sets of rooms have been empty.

In Tyndall's-buildings, unluckily, things have not yet worked well, financially. There are, however, causes that have produced this effect, which, when explained, should prevent those who take an interest in this movement from being disheartened. Other buildings in the hands of the Society pay a large per-centage,—the establishment in Charles-street, for example, returns more than ten per cent. The whole of the property, taking the average, made a return last year, exclusive of the cost of managing the Society, of four and a half per cent. ; while, as must not be forgotten, good accommodation was provided for a large number of persons on reasonable terms. The Society has been of great value, moreover, in distributing information to all parts of the kingdom. Praise to those who conduct it.

Although amongst the old the chance of a change for the better is not great, still we have hope that if proper exertions are used, we shall be able before long to act to some profitable extent upon the young.

Ill-arranged dwellings, want of proper education, and of honest employment for the children of the poor in our great cities, are the chief causes of crime and shortened life ; and it is difficult to know which of the above-named items is the means of producing the greatest amount of evil. Every one, however, will be doing good work who will improve the one and supply the other. It is clear that a certain amount of education will create a wish for better dwellings, and the improved homes will lead to an increased desire for advanced education.

If the improved dwellings which have been erected are not remunerative to the builders, or appreciated by those for whom they are intended, it is time to think of some other plan which may supply shelter to a large class that must be cared for.

In the National School hard by, the charge is from 2d. to 3d. a week for each pupil, and an extra penny or so a week is charged for drawing. Constituted as these schools are, and intended for the use of the children of our mechanics and persons of small means, whose boys are expected to take part one day in the production of some of our manufactures, it seems to be a question for the serious consideration of the managers whether it would not be advisable to abolish the extra charge for drawing,—a branch of education nearly as important as writing and arithmetic.

Along the valley of the Fleet, from Coppice-row to Farringdon-street, the work of demolishing old and rotten dwellings is being carried forward vigorously ; and on the opposite side of the street, a little to the south of the Clerkenwell Sessions House, many dwellings of a date anterior to the Fire of London have been removed. Bear-and-Staff-yard, Vine-street, and other old names of the streets west of the Sessions House, remind us of the time when they looked into the fields. It is interesting to stand now at Coppice-row and see the fine view of St. Paul's Cathedral which is opened out by the removal of these buildings. Eighteen or nineteen years since, it was by no means safe to venture into the neighbourhood which is now cleared. It was a dreadful place, filled to overflowing with the worst sorts of wretchedness and vice. When the removal of some of the houses in Field-lane discovered this comparatively unknown region to the sight of the thousands of passengers who pass along the great thoroughfare of Holborn, great was the astonishment of those who then came to take a peep at the unnatural-looking buildings which stood by, and in some instances were built over, the Fleet river. Many a story of Jack Sheppard, Jonathan Wild, and other well-remembered and not sufficiently despised vagabonds, was told to curious listeners ; with tales of murders and robbery ; of deceitful trap-doors, through which unwary visitors had been slipped into the

Fleet ; of bones and fragments of bodies buried in the basements of the dwellings. This run upon the place—bad as was the taste that prompted it—was attended with good, for many were thus brought to see dwellings such as they could not have dreamt of, and children and men of such a stamp as would make all, except the most thoughtless, shudder.

Here is an engraving that shows part of the remaining side of Field-lane. We went into some of the houses only a few days ago

Part of Field-lane, Holborn.

(February), and found that all we said of the place five years ago would still apply. Behind it there are houses in even worse condition.

If we cannot tell what has become of the population of the Fleet valley, we are, unfortunately, in no doubt about the place to which several of the *manufactories* have been shifted, and that is no farther off than Belle Isle, Maiden-lane. Here horses are melted, not in worn-out sheds such as those were by the Fleet, but in solid-looking buildings, which seem to be intended to carry on the work for years, independently of consideration for the health of the neighbourhood, public opinion, or the law. The smells which come from this district are sickening. If, however, you venture in the course of inquiry to mention to any manufacturer the complaints heard from the neighbours, you will probably be laughed at, and told, that "This is a *nuisance neighbourhood.* What business have you to interfere? Leave us alone—we neither hurt ourselves nor anybody else." Let us, however, say in reply, that what seems sport to him, is death to others. Many of the houses in this neighbourhood are in a most dilapidated and unwholesome state.

To turn from the swamps of this locality to a bridge. Near the bottom of Maiden-lane, or, as it is now called, York-road, an hospital has been commenced for the relief of the suffering poor of Camden-town, Somers-town, Kentish-town, New Smithfield, High-gate, and Islington. This still infant establishment was founded by, and carried on for six months at the sole expense of Mr. Statham, one of the medical officers; but as the number of out-patients had become on the average about 300 daily, and as many of these were pressing cases of disease and accident, it was resolved to enlarge the premises, and make them suitable for hospital purposes, for which more funds became necessary. These alterations have been carried out, and the number of attendances and patients show that such assistance is needed in this neighbourhood, although at a first glance one would think that the Free Hospital in Gray's-inn-lane would have been sufficient.

Feeling as all must the great need there is of medical assistance to a large class of the more moderately paid workmen and others, particularly those who have families of children, it would seem to be desirable to provide a department where persons of moderate means might, by monthly or quarterly payments, obtain efficient medical advice, without loss of self-respect.

Additions have been made recently to the Royal Free Hospital in Gray's-inn-lane. In the winter of 1827, a wretched female, under eighteen years of age, was seen lying on the steps of St. Andrew's Churchyard, Holborn-hill, after midnight, actually perishing through disease and famine. She was a total stranger in London, without a friend, and died two days afterwards, unrecognized by any human being. This distressing event being witnessed by Mr. William Marsden, the surgeon, who had been repeatedly struck with the difficulty and danger arising to the sick poor, from the system of requiring letters of recommendation before admission to the public hospitals, and of having only appointed days of reception; he at once determined, with the co-operation of several friends, to set about founding a Medical Charity, to which destitution and disease should

be sufficient introduction. On this principle the first Free Hospital
was established in Grenville-street, Hatton-garden.

It is satisfactory to learn that the poor do not seem to be unmind-
ful of the benefits received here, as is shown by the quantity of
copper coin (partly farthings) which finds its way into the little
boxes placed outside in the street to receive subscriptions. The pages
of the book in which receipts are recorded show, too, such entries as
the following :—" 2s. 6d. in thankfulness for first earnings, from a little
boy." " £2 from J. S. and half a sovereign, as a tithing to God and
his sick brethren." " A thanksgiving to God, from Matilda, 10s."
" £1. 1s. a free gift for legs and arms ;" while not long ago a poor
mechanic left at the gate of the hospital a brown paper parcel, which
was found to contain his watch, still ticking. In November, 1844,
a Bank of England note, of the value of £100, was found in the
subscription-box. On the enclosure was written—" Winter is coming :
Bis dat qui cito dat."

CHAPTER III.

PROFITABLE things for consideration are not necessarily pleasant
things. If silence is to be observed touching abominations which
demand reform, through fear of offending delicate sensibilities, instead
of pointing them out and denouncing them, the abominations will
remain to the end of the chapter. The first step towards obtaining a
remedy is to make the existence of the disease known. We must dive,
then, into the back-slums of London—the social morasses, the shadowy
corners—and bring into the light the one or two points of good and
evil found there during a recent walk. This time we speak not of
men's sorrows, but of the miseries which cows and sheep endure in
London, and the evils which result to the community in consequence.
London cows are, in many cases, kept in places where the poor
brutes are not only destroyed themselves, but are made the cause of
destruction to those living around. All who dwell near a cow-
keeper know the abominable smells which proceed from his sheds and
pollute the atmosphere during both summer and winter : there can
be no doubt of the unwholesomeness of such places. A number of
influential cowkeepers, acknowledging the evil, have formed an
association having for its object the improvement of the cow-sheds of
the metropolis. One of the regulations of this society is, that all the
premises belonging to one member shall be open to the inspection of
the others ; and that reports shall be made of bad conditions, with
hints for improvement when necessary. This is a praiseworthy step,
but one which will not be sufficient to satisfy the public.

In parts of the metropolis that we could mention, cows are kept
standing closely side by side in sheds placed in narrow lanes amidst

a crowded population. The pen is not so effective in conveying an
impression of such places as the pencil, so we give a view of a
"dairy," sketched on the spot in the heart of the metropolis, where,
as will be seen, families reside in the rooms above. The alley in

A London Dairy.

which it is situated is so narrow, that Scott's description of another
sort of locality in "Rokeby" will apply :—

> " For though the sun was on the hill,
>   In that dark dell 'twas twilight still."

Besides the unnatural gloom, confined space, and in some instances
want of drainage, the food of the London cows, which consists mainly
of grains and other refuse from the breweries, is not good ; and,
although it may increase the quantity, cannot improve the quality of
the milk. When we consider what an important part milk is of the
food of young children, it will be seen to be a matter of great importance.

Visitors to Smithfield towards the close of the market, may see
numbers of attenuated cows, blear-eyed, and with countenances
which are as unpleasant in their way to the sight as those of worn-
out habitual drunkards. The spines of the poor beasts are arched up,
and all the points of beauty and health are gone. These animals
have been bought chiefly from such cow-sheds as we have sketched ;
and many cows, when it is considered that they are no longer able to
supply milk, are not even fit to make an appearance amongst the
leanest kine of Smithfield market, but are taken away and *melted*,
or in *other ways quietly disposed of*.

It is painful to mention what is unpleasant, perhaps injurious to
individuals ; but feeling strongly the necessity of certain changes for
the public good, we are forced to place facts before our readers. It

would be better, if those who may feel aggrieved were to consider the times, and apply, without being forced, the means of improvement which increased knowledge has placed in their hands. Even when improvements can be easily made, however, and the necessity of them is acknowledged, it is long before a large number of persons can be induced to change. About thirty years ago, at Newcastle-upon-Tyne, with the exception of the statute fair, which was held three or four times in the year, there was no market for sheep and cattle; and the butchers were obliged to go every week to Morpeth, a place fourteen miles distant, where a weekly market was held. In order to get there, some of the butchers would start in the middle of the night, even in inclement seasons, to walk the dreary road. Instances have occurred of their being knocked down and robbed; and owing to the numerous calls for refreshment on the road, some were not sufficiently intelligent to make a very good bargain when they reached the market-place; many of the butchers travelled by stage-coach and other conveyances; but at the best, in wet and wintry weather, it was a lonely, uncomfortable, and expensive journey: and besides, when the sheep and oxen had been bought, they had to be driven fourteen miles home. Great was the grumbling, too, about the toil of these journeys, and often was it mentioned, in order to enhance the prices of meat. However, the population of the ancient town of Newcastle having much increased, the corporation determined to provide a weekly cattle-market close at hand, and it was curious to note how the butchers immediately set themselves in opposition to this, and gloried in the twenty-eight miles' journey, with all its expenses, inconveniences, and perils. For long the new market was left without either stock or buyers. In the course of time some of the most obstinate of the old butchers died off, and the advantage of the change became evident. Things advocated stoutly by parties in the metropolis at the present day, will cause, a few years hence, as much surprise as the conduct of the Newcastle butchers does now.

As regards the London supply of milk, time was when the slowness and difficulty of conveyance rendered it necessary that the dairies should be either in the metropolis or in the immediate suburbs; but the means of transit are now changed, and for fifty miles round this great city the cows can be milked at early morn, the milk brought by swift trains to town, and delivered at our doors in time for breakfast. It must be admitted that several of the London dairies, where capital is not wanting, are managed as well as the circumstances will admit of; but at best, the keeping of such animals in the midst of a huge population is bad, and should be discontinued.

Leaving the "dairy" (the words suggest a very different place, with "neat-handed Phillis" directing), we pass to some of the London slaughter-houses, and have illustrated the gentle means used to persuade the poor brutes to enter places altogether unfitted for the purpose to which they are applied. Measures should be adopted to put a stop to the tail-twisting and other barbarities resorted to.

A London Sheep-fold.

How Oxen are persuaded.

Our walk, when these were sketched, brought us to Lucy's-buildings, near the north end of Leather-lane, Holborn, and we inquired how matters were going on in that neighbourhood. At the time of a previous visit, the place was eminent for neglect and filth; and it was therefore with no small pleasure, that on reaching the approaches to it we found evidence of care. At the time of our call, some scores of costermongers and their assistants were carefully arranging their goods on trucks for the Leather-lane and other markets; and we could not help giving that

somewhat abused body credit for the exertions which they were
making to obtain an honest livelihood under circumstances of very
great difficulty.   It should be borne in mind that this class of the
London population are the means of not only preventing great waste
in the London wholesale markets, but of affording many little
luxuries to the poor.

Continuing in the same neighbourhood, we will look at an indi-
cation of a better time to come in Gray's-inn-lane,—a Social Bridge
which has been erected there.   It is but a small one, it is true,—but
a little hole will let in a deal of light,—a narrow causeway may save
an army.   This bridge takes the shape of a Ragged School, held at
No. 5, Fox-court.   It has little of the appearance of an educational
establishment, and would scarcely be discovered by those unaware
of its existence.   The basement consists of a dilapidated shop, part
of which is occupied by a mender of shoes.   On the rough planking
which has been put up to cover the rents of the window, are several
printed bills, setting forth that it is possible many residing in this
vicinity may not be aware of the ignorance, vice, and wretchedness
which prevail almost at their very doors, and inviting the well-dis-
posed to make an examination of this unfortunate locality, where
many families are so destitute, and many so degraded, as to.be un-
willing, or unable, to pay for the education of their offspring, and thus
be enabled to judge of the value of a ragged school amid the scenes
of squalor around,—a school which is constantly available for the
gratuitous instruction of these otherwise wild and undisciplined
children.

On the occasion of our first visit, the sleet and rain were pelting
down ; but this did not prevent numerous little boys and girls flocking
in from various directions, many of them without hats or caps, and
very badly shod : their faces and hands, however, in most instances,
were clean, and their hair in a good state.

Few could look at the order which here prevailed, and contrast it
with the manners in the homes from which the children come, without feelings of satisfaction.   A quiet word from the schoolmistress
seemed sufficient to still any disorder.

In addition to day-schools for boys and girls, and the evening
schools, the rooms are open on Sundays.   There is also a weekly
meeting for mothers, and a clothing club.

The large majority of those who reside within the Shadows of
London must be coaxed into cleanliness and order,—they will not be
driven ; and to the ragged schools and national schools scattered in these
benighted districts we must look to dispel the illusions and prejudices
which at present exist : they should therefore be well cared for, and
we hope that before long the school in Fox-court will be relieved
from difficulty.

Improve the homes, and teach the children, and we shall soon
lessen the numbers of the "dangerous classes," prevent much suffering and misery, and enable men and women to live out the term of

their natural lives, and to play their proper part in increasing the sum of general wealth and general happiness.

The poor cobbler who established the first ragged school should have a statue !

CHAPTER IV.

THE district of St. Jude, bounded by the Pentonville-road, Gray's-inn-road, and the Bagnigge-wells-road, is of singular character, and contains several thousand inhabitants.

Walking round the outskirts of the district, one cannot fail to be impressed by the number and size of the public-houses, which have the effect of making the ordinary dwellings look more dwarfed than they would otherwise seem.

The houses in St. Jude's are chiefly occupied by the industrious poor. In no part of London, of similar extent, will there be found so many widows, with families of children, struggling hard to earn a living by washing, ironing, and similar occupations. There is also a number of the better class of workmen with families, who are glad to avail themselves of houses at low rent : there are several coster-mongers, and but few who are absolutely idle.

Many would feel surprised at the immense number of children who throng the streets and back-courts of this neighbourhood, and it is fortunate that a ragged school is conveniently placed in Britannia-street. The Reformatory in the same street has been mentioned already.

"*Mangling done here.*"

Besides the ragged school and reformatory, the large training establishment, for children and teachers, of the Home and Colonial Schools is a great advantage ; and there is also the district church, in which are 500 free sittings.

On entering the boundary, the visitor will find within the line of high houses which surround it, numerous streets of houses of small size and two stories high ; the doors of some are not more than five feet high, and the rooms of size corresponding : they are built on the ground, in the same manner as those in Agar Town, and, even with good drainage, are very damp.

Many evils are increased by simple thoughtlessness. In the basements of some houses you may see the only window, not 3 feet wide or more than 9 inches above the footpath, covered up by an iron grating, placed in many cases not more than 6 or 7 inches from the front of the building.

Hundreds of people live below the surface of the London streets, in rooms to which such apertures afford the only means of light and ventilation. Small as is the limit here for light, that necessary of life, it is still further curtailed by bars of iron, more closely set than to any cell in Newgate.

Some would refuse to believe how many are born and die in these underground dens, into which a ray of sunlight can scarcely struggle. Here and in the garrets is to be found the largest amount of poverty. In addition to the want of light and air, these places are in most instances intolerably damp. The back kitchen is generally used by the numerous tenants in the house for washing: in many the cesspool-closet and dust-heap are placed there; and in eight cases out of ten the contents of the closet are passed under these places in badly-formed drains, that allow the gases to spread around, and quietly poison the inmates.

A systematic and general clearing of the undercrofts of London would add considerably to the wholesomeness of parts of the metropolis.

"Life," says Dr. Acland, "is a holy thing; and if communities throw away the lives of the individuals who compose them, or make these sickly, short, and miserable, the community will, in some manner, 'pay for it.' It will have work done badly by the crushed artisan while he lives; it will have to maintain him for years in his sickness, and his children on his death."*

We hope to hear before long that the Corporation of London have resolved to proceed with the erection of a pile of dwellings for the labouring classes, which has been long talked of. Some of the metropolitan parishes are becoming more and more overcrowded every day.

Let us in a parenthesis, by way of relief from the unpleasantness of the details we are forced to go into, here refer to the love of "art" which is often exhibited in the most miserable quarters, in the shape of plaster casts and little prints,—not of very refined character, it is true, but still agreeable and cheering as evidence of a striving upwards. The painted parrots and spotted cats, and red-and-blue varnished prints, which not many years ago *decorated* homes of greater pretence, have found a resting-place lower down in the social scale. Our sketch of an actual chimney-piece will serve as a record of some well-known barbaric favourites. Art offers itself as a social bridge of no ordinary size and strength.

Returning to the line we were pursuing,—It may safely be anticipated that great benefits will result from the labours of the various Officers of Health, who have been appointed under the Metropolitan Management Act.

* From "Health, Work, and Play," a valuable little tract.

It is, as we have again and again said, a plain matter of self-interest, as well as a solemn obligation, to exercise the most vigilant care in preserving to the poor their only worldly possessions—their health

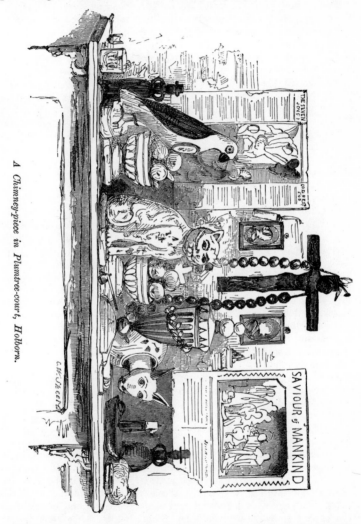

A Chimney-piece in Plumtree-court, Holborn.

and capacity for self-support: and this is the duty of the Health Officers.

If the whole population of London and its suburbs were placed under the same good circumstances as are the tenants of the Society for Improving the Condition of the Labouring Classes, thousands and tens of thousands of lives would be saved annually.

Thousands of lives! The fact is surely worth thinking over.

Endeavours are being made, in the metropolis and various parts of the country, to provide improved dwellings for the labouring classes ; but at present these are wholly incommensurate with the existing necessity.

In London various societies are at work, each in its little circle. The Lodging-house Act is working well, and the diminution of epidemic disease produced by it, is much greater than was even anticipated, and has contributed to the preservation of that portion of the population of the metropolis who have no settled place of abode. Still the evil is scarcely touched,—such is its vastness ; and we can put our finger on scores of localities which are a disgrace to a civilized country. Many of the fearful holes described in our earlier volume remain precisely as they were, hotbeds of disease and vice : some of them are even worse.

It is stated on the authority of the rector of one of the populous London parishes just to the north of the City, that there has been an addition of one thousand persons in his parish upon a former population of four thousand, since the last census, and *yet not a single house has been built* in the district : in fact, there is no room for building, every scrap of ground being covered. He says that people have been driven in from the dwellings destroyed in Holborn, Clerkenwell, and Spitalfields, and that they have been thrust upon the other population ; huddled into any hole and corner they could put their heads into,—not from poverty, but from sheer want of any dwelling within reach of their work ; that respectable artisans, particularly among the class who work at their own homes, even makers of little fancy articles and of parts of watches, have been forced into the same dwellings with some of the worst class, who have been driven from Field-lane and the "slums" near Sharp's-alley.

Good may be done and money made at the same time, or at all events not lost. We would just whisper, however, apart from this, without any desire to seem to affect the possession of the virtue we would see exercised by others, that " when God gives a blessing to be enjoyed, he gives it with a duty to be done ; and the duty of the happy is, to help the suffering to bear their woe."

Thousands of pounds may be saved by improved sanitary arrangements—and thousands of souls. Lord Shaftesbury has said that one-third of the pauperism of the country at large arises from the defective sanitary condition of large multitudes of the people, and that, if the population were placed under proper sanitary regulations, in less than ten years the poor-rates would be diminished to the extent of two millions annually. Who shall calculate the diminution also that would be effected in crime ? And crime costs a good deal of money, and causes a vast amount of suffering. To induce anything like the practice of morality on the part of men and women in the state of physical debasement to which thousands in this vast metropolis are condemned, is impossible, as we have asserted again and again. "Talk of morality," says Dr. Bickersteth, in a lecture on "The Physical Condition of the London Poor," delivered before the Church of England Young Men's Society, "amongst people who herd—men, women, and children—together, with no regard of age or sex, in one narrow, confined apartment ! you might as well talk of cleanliness in a sty, or of limpid purity in the contents of a cesspool. Look at the testimony of experience : I appeal to all who have ever laboured in scenes such as these—to our toil-worn parochial clergymen in metropolitan parishes—to our Scripture-readers and City missionaries, who have penetrated these haunts of infamy, and who are familiar with these nests of pauperism and vice—I ask if all their labour is not thrown away upon a population so circumstanced ? Does not the same state of things go on from year to year ? Is there any moral improvement in the mass, so long as the physical condition is unchanged ? I have put the question to men who have faithfully toiled for years in these dens of London, and the answer is invariably the same. No general impression is made. Here and there, possibly, one may be roused to some kind of moral perception, as by a miracle of mercy ; and what happens ? Why, the first token of moral life is an attempt to migrate, as though by the instinct of self-preservation, to some purer scene."

The Metropolitan Board of Works are about to form some new streets, in the construction of which many people will be turned out of their lodgings, and will be forced, unless proper provision be made, to flood the neighbouring localities. We would exhort the authorities to give this point consideration.

There is a great want of dwellings so arranged that the families of the better description of mechanics in the metropolis may live in becoming privacy, and be accommodated with proper conveniences and means for cooking, at a rental of from 5s. 6d. to 7s. per week. This amount several thousands of persons willingly pay for very inconvenient apartments. Should not capitalists endeavour to meet the requirement ? or, recollecting the passing of the Act of Parliament limiting liability, could not the London artisans do something for themselves ? Large sums have been collected amongst them for the purchase of freeholds in out-of-the-way places. Would it not be possible for them to organize societies for the erection of houses which might be well drained and ventilated, and divided into flats ? What can be done by means of association amongst the wealthy, is shown by the palace club-houses, where, for a payment which would seem inadequate for the provision of so much luxury, the members who choose to avail themselves of it have a splendid home. The problem how capitalists are to provide such accommodation as will be liked, with a pecuniary return, is not solved yet ; but we must not touch that point just now.

We have made two visits to a large tract of land known as Nova

Scotia-gardens, situated near Shoreditch Church, where a great change has recently been effected.

In passing along Old-street-road from the City-road in search of this place, the architectural features of the neighbourhood will be noted as peculiar. Many of the houses have been originally small buildings by the roadside, and the various alterations that have been made from

Nova Scotia Gardens, and what grew there.

time to time, to give them a more fashionable form, are curious. These attempts, however, have not been altogether successful; and the street, and indeed the whole of this neighbourhood, presents a more picturesque appearance than usual.

Here are several almshouses, which were erected originally amid the green fields.

We pass on, however, to Shoreditch Church, a short distance along

the Kingsland-road, to Union-street, on the right-hand side. This leads
to Crab-tree-row and Nova Scotia-gardens, which, notwithstanding
its fine name, presented, when we first saw it, the appearance shown
in the engraving, pointing to a condition of things not to be thought
of without astonishment and fear.

An artistic traveller, looking at the huge mountain of refuse which
had been collected, might have fancied that Arthur's Seat at Edinburgh, or some other monster picturesque crag, had suddenly come
into view, and the dense smell which hung over the "gardens" would
have aided in bringing "auld reekie" strongly to the memory.

At the time of our visit, the summit of the mount was thronged
with various figures, which were seen in strong relief against the sky;
and boys and girls were amusing themselves by running down and
toiling up the least precipitous side of it. Near the base a number
of women were arranged in a row, sifting and sorting the various
materials placed before them.

The tenements about were in a miserable condition : typhus
fever, we learnt from a medical officer, was a frequent visitor all
round the spot ; the water-supply was insufficient ; the drainage bad.
Since then a benevolent lady, whose charities have made her known
to the world—Miss Burdett Coutts—has assisted in appropriating
the vacant area more beneficially. The dust-heap has been removed ;
and, at one end of the land, a block of buildings, to accommodate, as
we understand, fifty-two families, is nearly completed. It is a lofty
pile,—too lofty ; and whether it is quite the sort of place that those
for whom it is intended will go to, handsome though it be, seems to
us somewhat doubtful. Most sincerely we hope that the fear may
be ill-founded. At any rate, it is desirable that the experiment be
tried before the other blocks contemplated be commenced.

The neighbourhood remains, at the date of this pamphlet, in the
most miserable condition, although both drainage and water-supply
have been in parts improved. At the back of Crab-tree-row, there
are courts of huts and hovels,—low, damp, and over-crowded,—which
produce the usual crops of illness, immorality, and premature deaths.
If proof be needed, consult the reports of the medical officer of
Shoreditch. The very name of the parish is suggestive of its early
condition.

Whether or not, as we have already said, the present experiment
is being made in the shape most likely to insure success, remains
to be seen. Certain, however, it is, that the first step towards effectually raising the condition of the very poor is to give them wholesome dwellings. Until they are taken out of the dirt, that brings
death, there is no chance of diffusing that intelligence—

> " Which binds us to the skies,—
> A bridge of rainbows thrown across
> The gulf of tears and sighs."

CHAPTER V.

WE once spent some hours in the Bow-street Police-court.

Bow-street is a name of power. The notion of a Bow-street officer still awes, though his red waistcoat is now scarcely remembered, and "the detective," not confined to that locality, has taken his place. Bow-street is the centre, or nearly so, of this great world of London, and its jurisdiction is over that miserable mass of humanity which festers round the plague-spots which have fastened on the very heart of our civilization. It is, *par excellence,* the London Police-office. And hence we see here brought to a focus all that is foul and all that is pitiful in the concentrated misery of the capital of the world.

There are few situations, indeed, in which a man can be placed, so trying as that of a London police magistrate. His position, if properly filled, calls for a union of qualities of the greatest and rarest order. His authority, in one sense, is absolute ; but for the control of the public press, the great mass of unfortunates who stand at his bar are absolutely at his mercy. He must be a sharp lawyer, with a memory capacious enough to contain an unknown number of statutes—elastic enough at the same time to admit the annual trifle of a hundred fresh ones cooked by Parliament. Every knave who comes before him has exercised his ingenuity in Lord Brougham's exercise of driving a "coach and four" through these enactments, and often with legal skill to back him. He must not swerve one hair's-breadth for any rank ; he must not give way to any false pity before an assumed penitence, or on account of a mawkish sentimentality. As the guardian of social order, he must at once be firm and composed,—ready to detect the specious tale of the bold, and yet shrewd, to elicit from the simple and bewildered what is necessary for their own defence. And all this must be done on the instant. When we think of the vast number of cases which are to be disposed of, and the varied circumstances by which they are environed, and at the same time observe how few important mistakes are made, we may justly be proud of this department of our national executive. The even-handed English justice dealt out by the metropolitan magistrates has now become proverbial. The men who fill these responsible stations have generally been well selected ; and the majesty of the law, while it has been vindicated, has won the respect even of the poor degraded beings whose evil courses have placed them under its ban. They know—and this knowledge is a powerful preservative from much evil—that if they break the bonds of society, they will meet the inevitable penalty, enforced without a shadow of oppression or vindictiveness, but with all the sternness which justice demands.

Within the precincts of Bow-street, the soul sickens, and it is hard to recognize one gleam of the pristine greatness in a mass which seems almost to have sunk to the level of the brutes. Care, hunger, disease, and crime have so acted upon many of them, that there is—

> " Not
> A finger-touch of God left whole on them ;
> All ruin'd, lost,—the countenance worn out
> As the garments."—MRS. BROWNING.

The newspapers daily report a selection of the cases which are tried throughout the different divisions, and there is no surer index of the need of home-mission work—no more melancholy evidence of the dreadful excesses of vice, than is presented by this fearful phantasmagoria of human life, seen in the columns of these prints. But lamentable as are these solemn evidences of blood, crime, and villany, they afford but a feeble idea of its amount.

On the particular morning of our visit, nearly as many cases were gone through as would suffice to fill a space equal to that occupied in the public paper by all the stations put together ; and that, too, on what would technically be called a " heavy " day. While we stood pent up in that little square dock, encircled by the dregs of humanity, who yet were brothers and sisters of the one great family, it would occur to the mind, as a fresh criminal was led to the bar, or some poor battered wretch staggered blindly forward to take the oath before she told of the savage treatment which had almost extinguished the spark of life, that one of the greatest of the Creator's mercies is the hiding of futurity. The most loathsome creatures that appeared had once been young and innocent ; but it was spared many of those who had reared and loved them, to behold the depths into which they should plunge. A snatch of the grand old Latin hymn forced itself upon us—

> " Dies iræ, dies illa,
> Solvet sæclum in favilla."*

We noticed the hard stern lines in the generally impassive features of the magistrate. Well, indeed, they might be so, for so great and terrible an experience as his is accorded to few. But sometimes even he showed the feelings which were roused. An expression of commiseration for some poor victim of brutality, whom the mad blow of frenzied passion, or drunken rage, had disfigured for life, if even that lasted. Or when some brawny hardened culprit came up to answer a charge for misconduct committed almost the moment he was out of

---

* Freely translated :—

> The dreadful day, the day of ire,
> Shall kindle up the avenging fire,
> Around the expiring world :
> And earth as sibyls said of old,
> And as the prophet king foretold,
> Shall be in ruin hurl'd.

prison, and human nature could not refrain from administering a stern rebuke where clemency was useless.

On the day in question (it was Monday) we were there for an hour and a half, and here is an epitome of the charges made :—1st, a woman—drunk ; 2nd, a woman, well-looking and decent—drunk ; 3rd, a man (a collector with the charity's money in his pocket)— drunk ; 4th, a boy—picking a pocket ; 5th, a woman—drunk ; 6th, a woman—drunk ; 7th, a man—case of stabbing while drunk (the injured man not sober) ; 8th, a girl of about sixteen—drunk ; 9th, a girl—drunk ; 10th, a well-looking woman—drunk ; 11th, a woman —drunk ; 12th, two boys (thirteen and fifteen)—for stealing : un-taught, with scarcely knowledge that they had done wrong ; 14th, a girl—drunk ; 15th, a woman—drunk ! How many more were brought up, victims of the monster evil—drink—we know not : it was too saddening to be endured longer.

But admitting that indulgence in intoxicating liquors is a monster evil, an overwhelming vice,— that it fills our workhouses, prisons, lunatic asylums, penal settlements, and churchyards ; demoralizes, debilitates, and degrades,—still, an objector may say, why introduce it here, when you are urging the evils of ill-arranged, unwholesome dwellings, and the want of sanitary arrangements ? For this reason, good friend, that a large portion of this intemperance and consequent crime is owing to the miserable condition of the dens in which the people are forced to exist. The impurity of the air creates a craving for stimulants, and the attractions of the public-house have no coun-terpoise at home. HOME ! As Southey says :—

> " There is a magic in that little word,
> It is a mystic circle that surrounds
> Comforts and virtues never known beyond
> The hallow'd limit."

But it would be difficult to associate " comforts and virtues " with the dens we are speaking of. Drink, moreover, is indeed a fatal swamp, engulfing millions of money and thousands of lives. And yet, sad to say, it makes for many the only bridge that offers itself to take them over the miseries of the day. Let us pity while we blame, and seek to teach rather than to punish.

Perhaps the best synopsis of the multifarious causes which exert so baneful an influence in filling Bow-street, and all such institutions, is to be found in two little volumes, entitled " Meliora; or, Better Times to come," being the contributions of many men touching the present state and prospect of society ; edited by Viscount Ingestre. They contain also a body of practical suggestions demanding consideration. Dr. Guy takes up the advocacy of that great system now receiving a trial, of which the result is being anxiously watched,—the policy of prevention. This broad principle is only now beginning to be appre-ciated. So long as we could export our criminals, whom we did not hang, so long we remained content on the old notion of " Out of sight out of mind." But by-and-by, when we found that the colonists objected to have their home made a receiving-house for the scum of others, then, when we were driven to keep the reprobates, whom we durst neither let loose nor send away, we began to think whether it were not possible to save them by some means from getting into that position at all. In a sanitary point of view Dr. Guy remarks, that to us the achievements of Cook, Howard, and Jenner, are very precious. With what irresistible arguments and potent precedents, have not the three sanitary philanthropists of the eighteenth furnished their successors of the nineteenth century! With what a treasure of analogies has not Howard himself endowed us,—analogies admitting of the most important practical applications! Mice are not more alike than the prisons of Howard's time and the low lodging-houses of our own day. Honest working men, by the thousand, in town and country, in every part of England, are compelled to live in as complete destitution of all the appliances of comfort and decency, and of all the physical aids to morality and religion, as the most degraded tenants of the worst gaols of the last century. They breathe the same foul atmosphere, they are pressed into the same narrow space, they are compelled to the same unseemly companionship, they languish under the same loathsome diseases, they are doomed to the same premature decay. Howard's gaol fever was but the prototype and progenitor of the typhus fever, which, one year with another, brings from fifteen to twenty thousand of the most valuable part of our population to untimely graves, and stretches twice as many for weeks together in muttering delirium on beds of doleful illness.

Sickened by such scenes as those we have depicted in Bow-street, we turn with a feeling of grateful relief to evidences that skilful and powerful men are awake to their obligations in their day and generation. That property has its duties as well as its rights, is an axiom, which, like many other axioms, has been very much left out of sight for a long time, all the more perseveringly, perhaps, because it is so very true and apparent. The " good time is coming,"—we hope it is not so very far off; but there is much to do: and as a fitting close to this chapter, we transcribe two of the genial verses of Martin Tupper, who affords another evidence on the point lately urged, that even in every-day concerns the poet has his use ; that it is, in fact, his office to lay down his choicest offerings on the shrine of common life, —home needs and home feelings :—

> " Still are these homes overclouded with night ;
>   Poverty's sisters are Care and Disease ;
> And the hard wrestler in life's up-hill fight,
>   Faints in the battle and dies by degrees !
> Then, let his neighbour stand forth in his strength,
>   Like the Samaritan, swift to procure
> Comfort and balm for his struggles at length,
>   Pouring in peace on the homes of the poor,

" Cleanliness, healthiness, water, and light ;
   Rent within reason, and temperate rules ;
Work and fair wages (Humanity's right) ;
   Libraries, hospitals, churches, and schools,—
Thus let us help the good brother in need,
   Dropping a treasure at Industry's door ;
Glad, by God's favour, to lighten in need
   The burden of life in the homes of the poor."

CHAPTER VI.

IF homes be looked into where the combined work of the family
will barely bring in, as is often the case, fifteen shillings a week,—
where the children are forced to labour at an early age, for prices
that are decreasing every time some panic produces dulness in
trade,—the question occurs, what is to become of those who are in
this way reared up to employment which is so unprofitable that it
will be out of their power, when they have arrived at years of
maturity, to obtain at it, single-handed, a sufficient living ? Money
aid in such cases is merely a temporizing.

The condition of the Spitalfields weavers and their families, for
example, is melancholy in the extreme : not only have the weavers
fallen into great poverty, but the winders of the threads and fol-
lowers of some other subordinate divisions of this once important
branch of English manufacture—women—can barely earn 1s. 6d. or
2s. a week. Of course, in such circumstances, these parties must
either starve or depend on extraneous relief. The sewing-machine
will no doubt effect a change in the business of both the needle-
women and tailors, who are already so much depressed that one feels
inclined to wish that this or some other invention may render the use
of human beings at such starving prices impossible. The engine
applied to watch-making will affect many. The employment of
children by capitalists in many fancy trades has been the means of
depriving many respectable females of half their income. It would,
indeed, require more space than can be given to mention the numerous
agencies which are at work, adding each month to the mass of wretchedness and destitution in our large population. It is, however, sufficient
for our present purpose simply to glance at the extent of the evil,
which must be remedied by the exertions not only of the Legislature,
but also of societies and individuals, and by leading workmen into
other and more profitable paths.

While looking at this dark and dreary aspect of London, we must
not omit to remember the sunny side of the picture—the improvement in the social position of the bulk of the people, and the great
increase of employment that has been brought about in other quar-

ters by those very changes which, during a transition state, have produced elsewhere much misery.

During the last twenty years a great change has taken place in public opinion respecting both sanitary and social reforms. The ragged schools are fulfilling their useful mission, and doing an amount of good that can only be estimated by those who have carefully examined the circumstances in which many thousands of the population are placed. The City Mission and other institutions; the exertions of district clergymen and surgeons, who not only do good in the practice of their vocations, but also by spreading a knowledge of matters which require change ; the national schools, the savings banks, and other associations connected with those most valuable establishments ; places of refuge for the destitute, and baths and wash-houses —are also working most beneficially. Still these helps are not yet sufficiently developed, and if they were, would fail to reach the bottom of the mass of wretchedness which has accumulated. More, especially, is needed in the way of wise assistance for those who at the present time, notwithstanding difficulties, remain honest, but who have little except begging, or worse, in prospect ; and it is a matter demanding inquiry on the part of the Government if the support of industrial schools and encouragement to a more extensive plan of emigration would not be a saving of expense to the country at large.

We require more ample means of affording a chance for the employment of those who have the inclination, but have had no opportunity, to work ; and while feeling the difficulty there is in leading youths who have been accustomed to irregular habits to change, it is certain that the most hopeful way is to remove them from the scenes to which they have been accustomed, and where they are beset with temptations on all sides. The sea, our infant colonies, and the army, are means that might be made much more available than at present for the purpose of placing numbers who would be otherwise lost to society in comparative comfort.

Although a change has been made in the system of training the children in some of the metropolitan workhouses, still great improvement is required in those, for the most part, frightful establishments, in order to fit both boys and girls to undertake appointments with chance of success. The masters and mistresses of some of the schools connected with the workhouses may be without fault, but it seems to us that in too many of these establishments in which there are large numbers of children, the latter are left in the care of ignorant persons, who have, perhaps, for nearly their whole lives, been accustomed to pauperism. It is not from such custodians that little children will be likely to learn lessons of perseverance and self-reliance. Anything more frightful than the condition of workhouse society can scarcely be imagined. In other respects, some boards of guardians might do much to ameliorate the condition of the very poor. We have seen instances of such treatment as to cause feelings of as much pity for those who could be so harsh and inhuman to suffering humanity, as for the unfortunates themselves. Many a family might have been saved from pauperism by a little kindly consideration on the part of those who have the management of the ratepayers' money. While saying this, it must be acknowledged that the attempts at imposition are numerous ; but we have seen cases in which the good and the bad have all been used as though they were not of the same species as those who crowded them into passages, and pushed and drove them like so many sheep and oxen.

Taking another road for a short distance,—as a matter of course, as the capital increases, the hovels and miserable houses in the suburbs give place to buildings of more substantial character, which are occupied by tenants of a better description. In Agar-town, King's-cross, the process of improvement is already beginning, and the substantial church and school there will, as the present leases fall out, be surrounded by rows of better-built houses, instead of those to which we have before directed attention.

It was not the fashion, two or three centuries ago, to build, even in the suburbs, such small and infamously slight houses as may be found in Agar-town, the Kensington Potteries, and many other metropolitan districts : yet the poor managed to get hold of the outskirts. These dwellings, in their turn, have given way to a fresh order of things. Other buildings have risen up, and the poorer classes have been driven to find abodes elsewhere. Some of them have gone to streets of decayed gentility, and rookeries as bad as St. Giles's have been formed in places which have the outward show of respectability.

It is curious to trace the decline of streets where, in Queen Anne's days, fashion and rank gladly took shelter. The first step in decline is generally the announcement that some professional gentleman has commenced business in one of the houses ; then some public institution is opened. On this the more aristocratic of the inhabitants move away, and in the course of time the street becomes entirely occupied by various establishments. After this a fancy stationer, or silk mercer, and other dealers, begin to fill windows with their goods. On this the higher class of professional men look for fresh quarters. The ordinary house-windows are made into small and second-rate shop-fronts, some of which are occupied by dairymen and beer-shop keepers ; then certain of the houses are let in tenements ; and rows of bell-pulls, some of them with small brass plates below, show that the dignity of the street is still kept up by persons who can each afford to rent a set of apartments. The decline still continues : the shops become occupied by small dealers in general stores ; even the bell-pulls gradually disappear, and a dense population, in most cases families living in single rooms, take possession of the street. This gradual succession of one rank after the other, and the desire as much as possible to follow those just a step above, are the result of a natural, and in some degree commendable feeling : but the practice is attended with ill consequences in a sanitary point of view ; these dwellings were not intended to be occupied by a multitude of families, and in the majority of instances the landlords take little care to improve them.

Generally speaking, independent workmen would refuse to wear the cast-off clothes of those above them, and yet they avail themselves in ninety cases out of a hundred of the cast-off houses of the upper classes, rather than choose houses which are in every respect fitter for the necessity of their own families. Workmen say they cannot find the improved accommodation they require, and builders refer to some of the model structures which have been put up, and mention the smallness of the dividend which is paid. It should be borne in mind, however, that extraordinary expenses have been incurred in the formation of the societies for improving the dwellings of the industrious classes, and that the cost of management and other charges are large. With proper arrangement, healthy homes may be built to pay the owner.

Amongst the curiosities of this question may be noticed the various neighbourhoods inhabited by foreign people, who have sought shelter amongst us at different times. There are the French emigrants of Spitalfields, the Italian refugees of more recent date in the district near Gray's-inn-lane, the Germans in close streets about Whitechapel, and the miscellaneous crowd who form a familiar feature of the streets near Leicester-square. All these groups from various nations have peculiar interest, but none of them, to our mind, are more worthy of notice than the Jews, the most ancient of all the London immigrants, who in large numbers gather together in Houndsditch and the parts surrounding.

It is worth notice as to the sanitary condition of the London Jews in poor districts, that, while fevers and other diseases have been cutting off numbers of their neighbours, the Jews have, to a remarkable extent, escaped the pestilence. This may be attributed to the care taken as to the use of wholesome food, and their attention to cleanliness. Besides, their practice as regards the interment of the dead is worthy of imitation; for not only do they provide burial-places outside the city they inhabit, but on all, except very rare occasions, the corpse is placed in the ground within twenty-four hours after death. It seems remarkable that, with such an example before them, many of other creeds should keep the remains of their friends in crowded dwellings for a week or ten days, and even a fortnight after death. This, however, is often caused by the difficulty of raising the money necessary for the expenses of the funeral. The Jews proceed immediately, on the death of a poor member of their fraternity, to raise a subscription of the sum needed, and it is not unusual to see a committee of Jews in the bustle of the clothes-market jingling a money-box, announcing the death of one of the trade, and collecting money, which amounts to a larger or smaller sum, according to the degree of respect in which the deceased was held. It is only some very notorious character or renegade who will not meet with this attention in time of need; and no poor Jew of Petticoat-lane can say a more cutting thing to another than " When

your father died, the box never went round for him." Other funds
are provided by letting some of the seats in the synagogue at a high
rent for this and similar charitable purposes.

Metropolitan taxation requires immediate revision. We have lately
been in several of the more neglected London streets, and, listening
to the opinions of persons of various classes, have found a strong feeling of discontent. The shopkeepers, taxed in some instances to nearly
6s. in the pound, must either raise the price of the food of the poor,
or, as they say, " go to the workhouse themselves."

It is not our object to discuss the causes which have led to conditions
so much to be lamented, but it is to be hoped that thoughts of the great
increase of pauperism in several parts of the metropolis will cause those
who have the power to aid in remedying the evil, and to consider that
the poorest neighbourhoods require the greatest amount of sanitary
care, and that the frightful condition of dwellings in these moral
swamps is a prolific means of filling both workhouses and prisons.
The high rates make parties willing to let houses to a " farmer," at
from £2. 10s. to £5. 10s. a year. Such circumstances are a means of
continuing the use of houses which are unfit for human occupation,
and we believe that the equalization of the poor-rates over the whole
of London would have the effect of encouraging persons to provide
improved dwellings in neighbourhoods where they are most required.
At the present time some of the inns of court, although surrounded
by large masses of the poor, are not called upon for parish rates—the
Bank of England, that wealthy corporation, is almost exempt—some
of the great dock companies have bought up an entire parish, and
are relieved from the poor—some rich parishes pay only about tenpence
in the pound for poor-rates ; and many other instances might be mentioned to prove the necessity there is for change.

Reference was made just now to Petticoat-lane. This locality last
session figured in Parliament. It was shown that vast numbers
of persons congregated there every Sunday morning, partly to traffic,
and partly for plunder. The Lord Mayor confirmed what had been
stated, and said he had been astonished to find that this was the
case. The readers of the *Builder* would not be astonished, because
they were told something of the place in that publication years ago.
The Lord Mayor said he had communicated with Sir R. Mayne upon
the subject, with the view of seeing whether the evil could not be
abated. But the House was probably not aware that Petticoat-lane
was peculiarly situated. It was a very long street, one half of which
was in Middlesex, and the other half in London ; and, unless the police
on both sides agreed upon one plan of action, the nuisance could not
be effectually dealt with. Booths of all descriptions were erected, and
a complete fair was held in that locality regularly every Sunday,
and attended by between 12,000 and 15,000 persons. It is another
example of those debatable lands to which we have drawn attention.

Petticoat-lane is famous for its market of second-hand clothes, from
those of the richest in the land to the tattered garments of poverty.

It must be seen in order to be properly understood. Such adventurous traveller as may wish to examine a large colony of an ancient and unchanged people, will do well by turning into Houndsditch from Bishopsgate-street, and then to the left along Cutler-street, and he will soon reach a large market, in which many of the most substantial of the dealers, male and female, have stalls and other accommodation. It is not a very easy matter, however, to reach this centre; for at certain times the approaches are densely crowded by Jew dealing with Jew, and the "tug of war," in the shape of loud words and energetic action, is startling. The contents of bags are turned out, and one piece of costume, after due eloquence has been used on each side, is exchanged for another,—boots and shoes for hats, or coats for trowsers.

There are parts of this marvellous metropolis where no clothes-man would think it worth while to enter,—even the exchangers of crockery and glass would not trouble themselves to call; but in these places "dolly shops" illegally advance money on such matters as pawn-brokers would not meddle with; and great is the interest paid for advances by the very poorest of the community. For the smallest sum up to one shilling, a halfpenny a month is charged, so that for the loan of sixpence they pay sixpence at the end of the year. From such shops as these, and from rag-shops, "goods" are brought to Petticoat-lane: even the articles which have been thrown out as useless, and are gathered in the street by the bone-seeker, find consideration in this neighbourhood: the upper parts of shoes, though the soles may be in a hopeless state; the soles or heels of others, from which the upper leathers have departed,—are sold to those who know how to dispose of them to skilful artists, who, by joining many portions together, will, if he may be believed, "make them better as new." Garments which, in the eyes of most persons, would seem to be quite useless, are eagerly purchased by other artists, who, with marvellous powers and chemical knowledge, turn, patch, and cleanse these cast-off habiliments, and put upon them a gloss that gives them a charm in the eyes of a future purchaser. Oh, strange and composite world!

In advancing to the central mart, the visitor will pass, as well as he can, through the crowd, without meeting with much notice, for all are too busy with their own pursuits. He will be surprised at the spirit of trading which is shown on all sides of him; an old hat is disputed about as if it were a matter of life and death. In the interior of the market a stranger attracts immediate attention; and if well dressed, has numerous communications made to him. The visitor seemingly in want of a coat is, however, the most attractive; and those who have experienced the rush of touters and porters at a foreign steam-boat station, may form some idea of the manner in which his attention is divided by the numerous offers. A man must either have an empty purse or great firmness to avoid making a purchase.

The immense quantity of goods here, suitable for markets at home and abroad, suggest that in London there is a greatness even in the

sale of old clothes. The busiest time is in the afternoon, from two
to five o'clock. Past this exchange, Petticoat-lane stretches in a long
line, and is generally thronged with dealers, some of whom carry on
their business in shops, while in front of them others pitch their
goods on the ground.

Being lately in this district on a Saturday evening, near the close
of the Jews' Sabbath, we were tempted to another examination of the
old houses which, on the east side of Houndsditch, differ so much
from the more modern buildings, and mark the margin of the Great
Fire. Looking up Cutler-street, the quietness which prevailed, recollecting the place on other days, was striking. The shops were closed.
Jewesses, many of them richly dressed, formed gossiping groups. In
Petticoat-lane the same observance of the day was general, and showed,
to some extent at least, the respect of this people for their Sabbath,
in spite of their love of gain.

Although the places of business (even the public-houses) were

nearly all closed, the place was thronged with such a multitude,
all in their gala costume, that some idea might be formed of the dense
population which occupies the surrounding neighbourhood. The
artistic observer would notice amongst the young girls faces of great
beauty, of that peculiar cast which has been transmitted from
generation to generation since the days of Moses.

Petticoat-lane is a narrow thoroughfare, from which branch off numerous alleys and courts. Most of the latter are reached by gateways, some of which are of very circumscribed width, and are generally built up at the extremity. The houses are small, the population is very large, and sanitary supervision is there required. Some of the pavements are in a miserable condition, and the drainage seems to be very defective. Hebrew-place appears to be still in a bad condition in this respect. Mulberry-court is very badly situated. The entrance is dark and narrow : beyond are thirteen or fourteen houses, and narrow avenues pass here and there, not so regularly, but in something of the same manner, as the cells of the honeycomb; and every part is swarming with life. While examining these back places as the darkness began to close in, and the gaslights and the stars to glitter, the noise rapidly increased. A change has in the course of a few minutes come over Petticoat-lane ; the shutters have been taken down, the windows lighted up, busy hands are at work displaying the merchandise ; costermongers with fruit and fish bring in their barrows ; from all sides throngs of working-men and others come in search of bargains ; and until a late hour of the night the busy exchange goes on. The scene is marvellous, and it might be useful if those who have the making of laws would visit such places, to glance at the thousands who are crushed together, and study the circumstances under which they are placed. There is something in the sight which of itself suggests the necessity of sanitary measures.

Let us say a few words under that head. It has been shown that Rose-alley, already alluded to, is the constant abode of sickness, and that not long ago it was infested with measles, which spread from house to house. This is not to be wondered at when it is found that in many cases the cubic space afforded to the occupants is less than 150 feet per head. It has been proved that each person consumes about 14 cubic feet of air per hour, and, by exhausting the vital element, oxygen, and producing carbonic acid to the extent of from four to five per cent., vitiates 100 cubic feet more. But the provision of this quantity would be so near upon the point of danger, that authorities are of opinion that even twenty times this should be supplied per hour. The prisoners at Holloway receive from twenty to thirty times this quantity, and the supply is not too large. In our public hospitals, from 1,000 to 1,700 cubic feet of space are allowed to each person, and when the area is lessened, injurious effects speedily follow. Dr. Bence Jones found that in the dormitories in St. Pancras workhouse, when only 164 cubic feet per head were allowed, the air contained about thirty times its proper amount of carbonic acid, and the closeness of the atmosphere was most oppressive, so that the inmates sickened of fever. Even in such of the barracks as have 500 cubic feet of space allowed, the air becomes charged with poisonous matter.

It is necessary to keep this important question before the public, and at the same time teach the multitude one of the most important means of promoting long life and health : most necessary, for notwithstanding all that has been done, it is, unfortunately, still the case, that by the large majority of people sanitary science is but little understood. Let us then aid elementary instruction by a few illustrations, not for the benefit of those who have studied the subject, but for those who have not given attention to this matter of life and death.

The annexed figure (1) drawn to scale, represents the 14 cubic feet of air which are used up per hour by each individual. This quantity of air, when returned from the lungs, exhausted of the vital element oxygen, is charged with carbonic acid to such an extent that it vitiates to a great and poisonous degree 100 cubic feet more of air.

IG. 1.

The adjoining sketch, drawn to the same scale as the former, contains 125 cubic feet of space, which is more than is provided for those living in Rose-alley and many other places to which we have directed attention. The figure A is a man of ordinary size compared with the cubic space provided in the dwellings in the alley ; and when we consider that in the St. Pancras dormitory, where 164 cubic feet were allowed to each person, Dr. Jones found that the air contained about thirty times its proper amount of dangerous carbonic acid,—as a matter of course the air in the dwellings in Rose-alley must be in a dreadful state of poisonous adulteration.

The next drawing represents a cubic space of 512 feet, a trifle more than the quantity allowed in the best of the London barracks.

The last engraving shows the proportion which 1,000 cubic feet bear with the above, and is the amount of space allowed in several hospitals. Even this is insufficient, without other arrangements : indeed, with 2,000 feet impurity gets in excess.

How, then, can we wonder at the loss of health, and the consequent excess of misery, in Rose-alley ? Once more, let it be remembered that impurity in air, and a miserable home, involve ill-health, degradation, and an early death.

CHAPTER VII.

IF we consider the enormous wealth of this country, and view accumulated property in a mass, as well as the huge fortunes which have been gathered up by individuals, it would seem that we are a thrifty nation. Unfortunately, nevertheless, in many points we are both careless and extravagant. It would be easy to give a long list of particulars which would explain our meaning, and show that in many instances those who had the means of preventing it have wasted human life by not making certain necessary provisions ; and that the industrious classes, the mainspring of the prosperity and strength of England, have not been sufficiently careful of themselves.

A change is coming over the management of our workshops and manufactories : the introduction of steam power, and the subdivision of labour—which has, in a great measure, been the result—have caused colossal establishments to rise up, wonderful to behold. Fifty years ago, a manufactory employing 100 men was worthy of notice : now we may travel over this land and see it thickly studded with works where from 1,000 to 2,000 hands in each are busily employed. Whether this concentration of human power will be eventually better for the working classes, or otherwise, is a question worthy of the most careful consideration, but which we will not now attempt to discuss. One thing, however, is certain, that some of these manufactories, including the men employed and their families, have a population of 3,000 or 4,000—enough to fill a small town. Amongst such important bodies of the English people, there should be provisions made of extent in proportion to the magnitude of the necessity.

In most cases the masters are anxious to do all in their power for the benefit and the improvement of the social position of the men, but they seem to fear being intrusive. The operatives are similarly sensitive, and so it is that little in comparison with what might be done is effected. In Lancashire and elsewhere, the masters and the workpeople have, in some instances, acted together in that kindly and wise way which is to the advantage of all parties ; but in the majority of cases this has not been done ; and there can be no doubt that many means of saving money, and adding to the comfort of the employed, are lost by the want of agreement between the great body of men and their employers.

In many very important establishments, no provision is made for sickness or accidents ; and yet how easy it is to establish a fund for that purpose. At Stephenson's (Newcastle), each workman pays a penny weekly, and with part of this sum a donation is made to the town infirmary, which gives the means of admission for a certain number to that institution, and the remainder of the money is distributed in weekly sums to those who require aid. In other places, where large numbers of persons are employed, some have moved in the right direction ; but nothing in proportion to the importance of the subject has yet been effected. So, believing firmly that, by system, the English workman may be able to provide for himself and family, in an independent manner, a cheap and whole-some dwelling, cheap and good education, and sound medical advice, we invite consideration to the subject.

It is worthy of note that the ribbon-weavers of Coventry are, to a considerable extent, their own masters. A large number possess looms which are worth £40 each and upwards. The purchase of such expensive matters by workers who, on the average, earn not much more than twenty shillings a week, is a remarkable instance of both thrift and industry. These looms are placed in various parts of the town, in rooms in the upper stories of houses, and during the last few years steam power has been applied to many of them by placing steam-engines in central situations, and then laying on the steam power as the water companies lay on water.

In some instances schemes of union and mutual assistance, similar to the freehold land and building societies, have been resorted to, and we are told that the value of the looms alone which are the property of the workmen amounts to £120,000 ; and to this £10,000 or upwards must be added for winding-engines, filling-wheels, jacks, and other machines. We shall be glad to find them extending their views to the purchase of dwellings.

At the Bank of England, the directors having provided a spacious apartment, Mr. Coe and some other leading men of that great establish-ment have in a most praiseworthy manner exerted themselves, and provided a valuable library, from which the numerous persons connected with the bank can, for a trifling sum, have books to read either in the place or at home. At the General Post Office, too, a library and reading-room have been established.

At the station of the Great Northern Railway, at King's-cross, where about 300 persons are employed, nearly 1,000 volumes of books were collected in comparatively a short time. The chief newspapers and other periodical publications are also regularly supplied. The charge per annum (not compulsory) for the use of the library, is to—

	In London.		In Country.	
	s.	d.	s.	d.
Guards, police, porters, and mechanics ..	1	6　....	1	0
Lad clerks	1	6　....	1	0
Junior clerks	2	0　....	1	6
All other officers and clerks	2	6　....	2	0

The reading-room for the clerks, and that for the guards, are furnished equally with the daily papers, and country members can have their books sent free to or from country stations if securely packed in brown paper parcels, and addressed " Library parcel, —— station, ——." In the larger reading-room, which is well adapted for the purpose, several good lectures have been delivered ; and it is to be hoped that before long this useful means of instruction will be resumed. It will thus be seen that by the payment of a little more than a penny a week, the mechanics connected with this railway may obtain a plentiful supply of excellent reading. It should be mentioned that, in addition to the ordinary members, honorary members are elected, who, being connected with the establishment, pay a certain sum, or give books or papers of that value.

In connection with the Great Northern Railway, the Sick and Funeral Allowance Fund should not be passed over. It was established in 1853, under the following circumstances. After several interviews with a deputation of seven, representing the several classes of guards, police, porters, &c., with the secretary and general manager, a meeting was appointed to be held at King's-cross, in June of the above year, of the directors and officers and servants of the company, when it was determined to establish a sick and funeral allowance club, to be ruled as follows :—

The classes required to contribute to this fund are—station inspectors, guards, police, and porters. Any other officer or servant of the company may do so, on his application to that effect being complied with.

The contributions are divided into three classes.

The fourth rule states that, " Under all circumstances, so long as a man continues in the service of the company, there shall be deducted from his wages the sum per week, according to his class, as follows : —Class A, 11d. per week ; Class B, 9d. per week ; Class C, 7d. per week." These sums, at a glance, seem high ; but the advantages are considerable.

The last rule states that this fund shall be administered under the authority of the board of directors, whose decision shall be binding on the parties in every case. No doubt the enforcement of payment is in many instances a great benefit ; but in cases such as this the workmen should have a voice in the management of money which is taken from their own earnings. Why not, in connection with this and similar establishments and manufactories, let the management rest in the hands of, say, seven of the representatives of the workmen, and two or more of the heads of the concern ? Good would result from such periodical mixing together of various classes—in building a Social Bridge.

It is noticeable how many, eminent in the various walks of science, men famous in literature, presidents of societies, editors of newspapers, managers of large establishments, and even aldermen of London, are from the provinces. The deteriorated condition of the atmosphere in town, the great cost of rent and living, and the want of good and sufficiently cheap education for the industrious classes in this wonderful community, make it difficult to a certain extent for a large portion of the youth of London to gain the amount of physical energy and proper knowledge necessary in first commencing the business of life.　Those acquainted with the condition of the London artisans, even of the better class, know the trouble there is in getting their sons bound to a good trade : in many instances either premiums are required, or a considerable portion of the boy's time is given for small sums : often two or three years pass without wages. The expense of this to persons of limited income is great, and the only chance, frequently, of rearing the family is to get one or two of the eldest apprenticed, and the rest sent to situations as errand-boys, and to other positions from which they seldom rise to much usefulness. There are many other circumstances that in London prevent thousands from being provided with that valuable faculty—the means of earning a livelihood by the possession of skill in an honest trade,— and which we must pass over, in order to direct attention to one chief cause of the advantage the youths of the provinces have over those of the metropolis : this is, the means of association amongst those following similar pursuits of the ages between fourteen and twenty-one.

In London, such is the state of society, that very often people are not known to their next-door neighbour ; and many are completely at a loss how to employ the spare hours of the evening in improvement. In the country towns, bands of young men, similarly circumstanced, meet at each other's houses, get attached to the Mechanics' Institute, and, by a friendly rivalry, make progress.

Much might be done by the young men of London themselves. In many instances the proprietors of manufactories could, without much trouble, allow a room as a place of meeting for the apprentices, three or four evenings a week.　Masters ought to direct the attention of their lads to the importance of the improvement of their leisure hours.

We should be glad to hear that the clergymen and other leading persons in each of the new divisions had given careful consideration to the amount of education required amongst the young workmen of their neighbourhood; and to the mode of assisting self-supporting institutions.　They could then learn the general feeling by visits throughout the districts, and by calling public meetings of the working classes in school-rooms and in other convenient places.　The clergy of the last generation have some remissness to answer for in this respect.

In watching carefully the growth of institutions which have for their object the advancement of the great masses of the community, there are few evidences of decided progress which afford more pleasure and seem more pregnant with important results than those educational establishments for adults which are rising up in all the districts of the metropolis.　In these places, many of them humble enough, lectures are delivered on popular and instructive subjects by men of ability and respectable position. Classes of rudimentary and more advanced description are formed, where those who have been unfortunately neglected in younger days, may, with pleasure to themselves, and without loss of self-esteem, acquire the mechanical means of education.

When we consider that, although a great amount of good results from the working of the national schools, it is not one scholar in ten who obtains what may be called a sufficient plain education,—that is to say, skill in English reading, a thorough knowledge of the first leading rules of arithmetic, the principles of grammar, and the faculty of writing a fair and legible hand,—the necessity for adult schools is evident.

The failure as to the useful education of the thousands of the children of the industrious and poorer classes, who depend on what is called the national system, is not to be attributed so much to imperfections in the system itself as to the want of regular attendance of both boys and girls; and yet, after very careful observation, we are forced to say, that although those who have been regularly at school—say from seven till thirteen years of age—may have acquired a large amount of general knowledge, such as the principles of astronomy, natural history, and geography; yet a far too large proportion are deficient in the simple acquirements alluded to, which should be made the basis of all education.

The large number of the imperfectly educated who crowd to the adult schools that have suddenly sprung up, shows that a good spirit exists amongst the youth of our large towns, and it will be promoted and increased by example. They who have been neglected—in most instances by no fault of their own—should seek out these working men's educational institutions, and not be ashamed to begin at the beginning. Let them recollect with encouragement that George Stephenson could not read a letter in a book until he was eighteen or nineteen years of age, and grown to the stature of a man. Let them bend the strength of their minds to the means of obtaining the information and skill required in their own business; remembering that the concentration of mind on a particular subject is a main secret of success.

And what is being done for the other sex? Little or nothing. And yet—

> " The woman's cause is man's. They rise or sink
> Together. Dwarf'd or godlike, bond or free;
> If she be small, slight-natured, miserable,
> How shall men grow ! "—TENNYSON.

The difficulty of obtaining profitable employment for a very intellectual portion of the women in large towns is shown in various ways: for instance, a few months ago, in reply to an advertisement in a London paper, seeking a young person as useful companion to a lady, at a very moderate salary, there were 270 applications in a few days. The managers of the Electric Telegraph have very wisely adopted the employment of female clerks, who are found to answer the purpose admirably; and this, when the resources of the great invention have been fully developed, will be the means of affording occupation to some thousands of young women.

The condition of the needlewomen in London is known to be deplorable; but only those who have seen it with their own eyes can fully appreciate the misery which at present exists. It is a melancholy fact that, as matters are working at the present time, large numbers who would willingly earn their food by honest industry are yearly falling into greater poverty; and it is unfortunately the case in other trades besides that of the needlewomen, that the rich capitalist is getting richer, and the poor workman and workwoman poorer. It would require a large amount of space to discuss the causes of this unfortunate state of affairs, and the different views of this important subject which are held by those whose opinions are worthy of consideration. It is not our present purpose, however, to do so. We have a different object in hand at this moment.

Those who have examined with care the various phases of London life, will appreciate properly well-intentioned plans having for their object the provision of arrangements to enable members of different classes to escape from inconvenient and too often dangerous conditions, and to improve the means of living, with comparatively limited income, in comfort and respect in this metropolis. These are to be placed amongst Social Bridges: all honour to the builders.

There is an institution of this kind to which attention may be directed. It is situated at No. 44, Great Ormond-street, that somewhat stately remnant of Queen Anne's days, which has declined somewhat in the manner we have elsewhere sketched. The house was formerly the residence of Lord Thurloe, and is a characteristic specimen of the London domestic architecture of the time. So far as the interior arrangement is concerned, it has considerable elegance; the entrance-hall, with marble floor, wide carved staircase, ornamented panels, and ceiling of rich design, are noticeable: the lighting of it is excellent: the rooms are lofty: the dining-room, on the ground-floor, is adorned with columns, and is a handsome apartment, in which have assembled many an eminent company in former days. Other rooms lead to a terrace, communicating with a large garden, which, by the way, might be made a little more trim than it is.

Large and comfortable, though old-fashioned, this mansion contrasts well with many places in which some thousands of the young women of London are by force of circumstances obliged to lodge. Amongst the female part of our population, a large number obtain employment in the establishments of milliners and dressmakers both at the west end of the town and in the City: in some instances lodging is provided for the assistants and learners: in others they are obliged to find sleeping-rooms themselves. Of course many young women so employed have the shelter of the homes of parents and other relatives: there are, nevertheless, a considerable number who, with slender means, are obliged to provide for themselves.

Well, then, it must be evident to every one, as matters are at present, that a respectable establishment, managed in a right manner, by those who can command general confidence, for the use of young women who have not a proper and comfortable home, must be of great service. Besides the workwomen who are reared in London, there also come, year after year, hundreds of dressmakers, and others, from the provinces, to seek improvement here, for the purpose of enabling, them to commence business in their native places with a better chance of success ; and the necessity of some provision for these classes different from that generally obtained, is so evident, that we need not say more on the point. This necessity seemed so great to Lady Goderich (now the Countess of Ripon) and Lady Hobart, that they determined to risk the expense of opening a house in Manchester-street, to supply the want ; and after trying the experiment there for some time, they took the house we are now speaking of, where young women can find a home, after their labours, at a cost of from 2s. to 2s. 6d. a week each. Lord Thurloe's dining-room is used as a sitting-room by the inmates, and in it there are a pianoforte, a good library, and other means of amusement. A Lady-resident, who appears heartily earnest in her task, manages the house, and arrangements are made, something on the club principle, to provide meals at a cheap rate. The house would accommodate upwards of sixty, and it seems to us that the advantages of this home only require to be understood by those for whose use it is intended, for the establishment to be fully appreciated. In the meanwhile the expense is great to the ladies who have made the experiment, and it is desirable that the place should be made known. At the present date (Feb., 1859), the house, strange to say, has only twenty-one inmates ; some prejudice, or misconception, tending evidently to prevent entry.

CHAPTER VIII.

As the education and the training, so are the children ; as the children, so are the men and women. If, for example, we would have the sons of the struggling classes grow into orderly, sensible, and striving citizens, we must give them a road out of the slough, show them the value of order, and furnish them with weapons for the strife ; and, to confine ourself to two points out of many, if we would have the easy classes hereafter, the well-to-do, alive to excellence, tasteful, and appreciating beauty, care must be taken that the senses of the children are early accustomed to beautiful forms, colours, and sounds. As poor Loudon used to say years ago, the infant-school is the lever by which the improvement of society must be worked. Every effort to provide means of training for those who would otherwise be without it,—every endeavour to give the children of the poor some knowledge of common things, and lead out their better parts, has our heartiest support. Let us offer a word of thanks, then, to Mr. Robert Hanbury, M.P., who is aiding to form a laundry, where girls may be received and instructed in such operations as would enable them to undertake engagements either in families or in washing establishments, or as wives. It is proposed that the girls should be properly cared for, and receive necessary teaching of other descriptions. A building has been taken, known as West-end House, situated between Kilburn and Hampstead, and additions have been made to it to fit it for the purpose. Seven girls have been received, and subscriptions are asked for.

The great need of means for instructing young women in the proper execution of work which will enable them to earn an independent and respectable livelihood in all our large towns, is evident; and several attempts have been made to provide this teaching for those whose homes are such that they have no opportunity of acquiring there the knowledge and facility which would enable them to do their duty properly in decent families. This want leads many girls, who are afterwards to become the wives of working men, to flock to the various departments of needlework, and to such fancy occupations as bugle-threading and artificial-flower making, which so occupy them through some of the most useful years of their lives that they seldom have much liking for or know anything of the household duties necessary for the comfort of a family. Businesses of this kind give employment to large numbers of young children, but *profitable wages to very few adults*. For instance, girls are sent to assist in the manufacture of artificial flowers as young as six or seven years of age. The bulk of the work is mechanical, and can be easily acquired with but little practice. On the design of a flower being determined, the die-sinker is set to work to engrave stamps, which, with the aid of a machine, strike through several sheets of muslin, or other material of the required colour, at the same time, the forms of the leaves or parts of flowers. The staining process varies some of the pieces, which are then distributed amongst the little workers. For instance, having all the materials for a number of violets prepared, some of the girls are provided with pieces of wire cut to the proper length, and these are covered with green paper, which has been already cut in strips : the petals of the flower are fixed to the top of the wire, and the other parts are rapidly gathered up and put in order, when it is passed to a superior hand, who pastes the whole together and fashions it into shape. The staining of parts is not difficult, and the chief aim in this work seems to be to produce the greatest quantity in the shortest time. We are told that fresh designs, both single flowers and groups, are occasionally purchased in Paris, and then reproduced in London in a superior manner, and at a less cost than they can be made in quantities in the French capital. It might be thought that those employed in this manner would have some knowledge of botany, and take an interest in the exact imitation of nature. This, however, is not the case ; and many who have worked long at particular flowers are totally ignorant of their names and peculiarities. They simply work in putting together so many forms which are already cut. The bulk of our readers know as little of the system pursued in making such things, as these young London workers know of the flowers they imitate; and what we would show is, that sending children of tender years to this and similar employments prevents them from acquiring the knowledge necessary for useful life. When the demand is brisk, they may earn from ten to twelve shillings a week; but constant employment is not always to be had, and, taking into account the time lost, it is probable that the average wages of this class is not more than eight shillings a week thoughout the year,—a small sum to provide lodging, food, and clothing. Moreover, the wheel of fashion may turn, and artificial flowers, as an article of female adornment, may become as little in request as are the richly-ornamented brass buttons which were once the glory of all true-born Englishmen.

Returning to Mr. Hanbury's laundry, we must note that there are difficulties in the way. At the foundation of the institution for destitute persons, near Field-lane, arrangements were made to provide the means of teaching girls who had been reared under bad conditions the art of spreading a table-cloth and arranging a room with neatness, to wash and iron linen, and so on; but the endeavour, although feasible in theory, did not succeed. Habits of neatness and cleanliness are not to be bestowed in a dozen lessons; moreover, there was a want of materials to work upon, and the whole had the aspect of a "make-believe." The laundry, which, it is necessary to say, has a much more promising appearance, should be made as nearly self-supporting as possible, and have such a character as may induce respectable working-men to send their daughters for the instruction that would be afforded.

High up in a house in Percy-street, Rathbone-place, an attempt is being made by an earnest woman to employ and improve a few girls. What she seeks is by the manufacture of toy-furniture, during one half of the day—tables, chairs, beds, and sofas, mostly formed of wire, covered with various materials—to enable them to maintain themselves; and, during the other half of the day, to acquire some useful knowledge. The endeavour has not reached very far yet: the sale being comparatively limited, the number of girls is at present very small. The toys will be found at stands 59 and 60 in the Soho Bazaar. These are more tasteful than some of the toys sold for children, and not dear. Aid is deserved.

And this brings us to the second point of our observations. Toys ought to be made to advance education; whereas the majority of those furnished to children in this country must do a great deal more harm than good: half of them should be burnt ignominiously as early corruptors of public taste. It is impossible to estimate the extent to which the after-life is influenced by the earliest impressions. A child should see none but beautiful forms.

Foreign toys are generally much better than English toys. Look through a collection of the latter : you will find them flimsy and inartistic in the extreme ; many of them hideously ugly, others made as if expressly to break—an evil in more ways than one, since they may actually engender a habit of destroying. Some of the toys in the German Bazaar display considerable artistic power : many of the small heads, for example, used as boxes, are forcible and clever ; and there is a French infantry soldier rude but characteristic. The carts and drays are exceedingly well made, and the horses full of spirit,—unlike the barrels. Some of the best toys obtainable, "Noah's arks," for example, are made in Switzerland—in picturesque mountain regions : most of the animals are cut in soft white wood, and some are beautifully formed, with special disregard, nevertheless, to proportionate size. Whole families employ a large amount of their time in this manufacture. One man is famous for his antelopes, another for lions, some for cats and dogs ; and we are told that they often go on, from boyhood to old age, carving dogs or lions as their taste may have led them to either one or the other in the first instance. Some toys seem to have afforded employment for several generations, and it is noticed that the well-known gaily-painted Swiss milk-maids and similar figures have not been altered in form in the smallest degree for upwards of a century.

In many articles deterioration is evident : compare the nut-crackers to be found in some of the toy-shops, with two common specimens we have sketched, which were made—one early in the reign of Queen Elizabeth and the other in the time of Charles II. These are not remarkable for purity of design or beauty of workmanship, but they show that quaint feeling which existed in former days, and which caused our workmen to adapt with different degrees of finish picturesque and artistic forms to the most ordinary objects. They serve also to mark in some measure the change which took place in a certain interval. In the older may be seen a remnant of the Mediæval spirit. The bird in the foliage picking the nuts well carries out the idea of the head-piece and jaw. On the other, beyond the head, there is no attempt at that kind of decoration which conveys any idea.

In the old days, the English people were not so fortunate as to have our famous contemporary *Punch* to cater for that quiet feeling for fun (which, in spite of all that has been said to the contrary, exists in this country to a remarkable extent), and to figure in a humorous yet philosophic manner the follies and abuses of the age. The spirit, however, which has led to the appreciation of *Punch*, showed itself in various other ways—in the carved stalls of cathedrals and churches, the cunningly devised rebuses, and other portions of ancient architecture.

In examining the table vessels of the Middle Ages, all must be struck by the extent to which the feeling of design has been carried. Amongst these may be noticed vessels shaped like bears, lions, and other animals, the crests of distinguished families, and which, when filled with the beverages of those days, were almost as powerful in the overthrow of man as the animals represented. Great ingenuity was displayed in the construction of drinking-cups, both those made of metal and of clay. Some are so contrived with holes, that if the thirsty soul do not understand the trick of the tankard, he finds the contents spilled upon the habiliments instead of entering the mouth ;

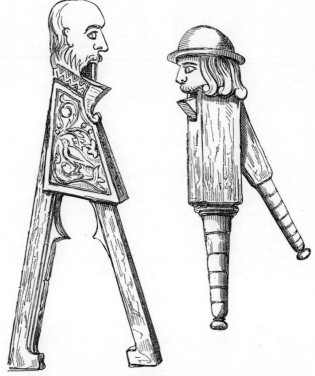

Nut-crackers: Time of Queen Elizabeth and Charles II.

and some are so made that when the jug is emptied, a peculiar and unpleasant croaking sound is heard, and the astonished drinker is still more surprised by the appearance of a frog, or some similar animal, with uplifted head and open mouth, at the bottom. Some of these flagons are in the shape of windmills, and others of human figures, the head and parts of the body of which can be lifted up, to serve the purpose of lids. Some cups are made without stands at the bottom, and can be replaced on the table only when the contents have been emptied. We might mention many other instances of the description of design above referred to, the "grey beards," and devices on bottles ; but it is not necessary, nor to direct attention to the beautiful design and workmanship of the period referred to, exhibited in objects more important, conceived and executed with a more refined and a higher feeling. We are dealing with toys and their manufacture,—a business of enormous magnitude, and concerning which much might be said. Our object, however, now, is simply to urge, as we have more than once done before, that the toys of children offer a ready means of education, and probably exercise an important influence on the career of thousands. Some would have us leave the taste of the young to take its chance. " Thelwall," says Coleridge, " thought it very *unfair* to influence a child's mind by inculcating any opinions before it should have come to years of discretion, and be able to choose for itself. I showed him my garden, and told him it was my botanical garden. ' How so ?' said he ; ' it is covered with weeds.' ' Oh,' I replied, ' *that* is only because it is not yet come to its age of discretion and choice. The weeds, you see, have taken the liberty to grow, and I thought it unfair in me to prejudice the soil towards roses and strawberries.' "

" Roses and strawberries !" What a pleasant sound the words have : what soothing, healthful visions they conjure up. What a goodness it was that gave us flowers, and made us love them :—

> " Our outward life requires them not,
> Then wherefore had they birth ?
> To minister delight to man,
> To beautify the earth."

Pleasant things, with pleasant thoughts for all : profusely scattered —cheap enjoyments ! Flowers, before now, have formed the bridge to give means of escape to the pent-up and care-oppressed spirit—

> " What more than magic in you lies
> To fill the heart's fond view."

The Smoke Act is giving flowers to London, and their humanizing and refining influence will lend its aid for the general advancement.

CHAPTER IX.

THE connection between disease and defective structural and economic arrangements continues to demand the most serious attention. The relationship of cholera, and fever, and crime, to cesspools, imperfect drainage, impure water, overcharged graveyards, and want of ventilation, is a great sanitary question, with which we feel ourselves all the more urgently called upon to deal, to the best of our ability and experience, since it is one on which the medical faculty themselves, strange to say, differ materially.

This is an unfortunate state of things, and shows the necessity for renewed and continued inquiries.

One thing appears beyond all doubt,—and it is on this we work resolutely, however feebly,—that where human beings are crowded together in ill-arranged dwellings ; where the drainage is bad and the cesspool lurks ; where refuse rots, the air is vitiated, or the water impure and scanty,—there cholera and fever, when evoked, reign and slay.   Those still speak correctly who make King Cholera sing,—

" What is my court ?   These cellars piled
    With filth of many a year ;
These rooms with rotting damps defiled ;
These alleys where the sun ne'er smiled,
        Darkling and drear !

These streets along the river's bank,
    Below the rise of tide ;
These hovels, set in stifling rank,
Sapp'd by the earth-damps green and dank ;
        These cesspools wide.

These yards, whose heaps of dust and bone
    Breathe poison all around ;
These sties, whose swinish tenants, grown
Half human, with their masters own
        A common ground.

What are my perfumes ?   Stink and stench
    From slaughter-house and sewer ;
The oozing gas from open'd trench,
The effluvia of the pools that drench
        Courtyards impure."

Two points have been often dwelt upon by the Registrar-General in his reports, as increasing the risk of cholera, namely, lowness of level and impure water.   Thus, after pointing out in one of his reports, that the district in which the poorer classes abound suffered generally most from the epidemic, he said : " From an attentive consideration of all the facts, the rich, living on low ground, in houses supplied with impure water, are in great danger during a cholera epidemic ; while the industrious, hardworking population, living on simple food, in clean houses not much crowded, supplied with pure water, on high ground, or on well-drained ground that has not been a marsh, have little to fear from cholera in England."

Contrasting some of the districts, the Registrar has said : " Rother-hithe and Chelsea differ little in rental; but the Chelsea district, supplied by the Chelsea Water Company, is on an elevation of 12 feet, and lost 47 inhabitants in 10,000 by cholera ; while Rotherhithe, on lower ground (0 feet), supplied with impure water, lost 176 by cholera in 10,000 inhabitants.   In Hackney, again, the people are apparently not in better circumstances than the people of Camberwell, yet in the two epidemics cholera was fivefold more fatal in Camberwell than it was in Hackney ; Camberwell lying low, and receiving the impure water; Hackney lying high, and receiving, in 1854, a water of better quality."

Touching impure water, the late Dr. Snow, who died too soon, considered that the morbid material producing cholera must be introduced into the alimentary canal—must, in fact, be *swallowed*, and that it has the property of reproducing its own kind. Particulars of the *way* in which it is swallowed would scarcely suit these pages : suffice it to say, that the want of personal cleanliness, scarcity of water, deficiency of light, and over-crowding, are shown to concur in bringing this about; and his theory is made to explain why in thousands of instances a case of cholera in one member of the family was followed in hundreds of instances by other cases, whilst medical men and others who merely visited the patients, escaped. The chief means of extension, however, he considered to be the contamination of the water, used for drinking and culinary purposes, by matters, containing the morbid material, either permeating the ground, and getting into wells, or by running along channels and sewers into the rivers, from which entire towns are sometimes supplied with water. The cases where attacks of cholera were traced to the contamination of water by adjoining cesspools, are not few.

When the terrible outbreak of cholera in Broad-street, Golden-square, and adjacent streets, of which we have had occasion to speak, took place, Dr. Snow suspected some contamination of the much-used pump in Broad-street, near the end of Cambridge-street; and he brought together a number of circumstances which seemed to show some connection. Of the eighty-nine deaths from cholera registered during the week ending Sept. 2nd, in the sub-districts of Golden-square, Berwick-street, and St. Ann's, Soho, he found that nearly all had taken place within a short distance of the pump. There were only ten deaths in houses decidedly nearer to another street pump, and in five of these cases the families informed him that they always sent to the pump in Broad-street. "There are certain circumstances bearing on the subject of this outbreak of cholera which require to be mentioned. The workhouse in Poland-street is more than three-fourths surrounded by houses in which deaths from cholera occurred; yet out of 535 inmates only five died of cholera, the other deaths which took place being those of persons admitted after they were attacked. The workhouse has a pump-well on the premises, in addition to the supply from the Grand Junction Water-works, and the inmates never sent to Broad-street for water. If the mortality in the workhouse had been equal to that in the streets immediately surrounding it on three sides, upwards of 100 persons would have died."

At a brewery in Broad-street, where there were seventy men, none suffered from cholera : few drank water at all, and the few who did, never obtained water from the pump, having a deep well on the premises.

Dr. Snow gave a map of the locality, showing the deaths by a black line in the situation of the house where it occurred, and adduced reasons for believing that the deaths either very much diminished, or ceased altogether at every point where it was decidedly nearer to send to another pump than to the one in Broad-street. Against one of the houses, immediately adjoining the pump, there are eighteen black lines! The total number of deaths ascertained was over 600! The pump-well was afterwards opened, and its connection with a cesspool was shown unmistakably.

Some extraordinary facts have been deduced from an examination of a part of London where many of the houses are supplied by the Southwark and Vauxhall Company, and others by the Lambeth Company, who take their supply at Thames Ditton. The pipes of each company go down all the streets. "Each company supplies both rich and poor, both large houses and small: there is no difference either in the condition or occupation of the persons receiving the water of the different companies. Now it must be evident that, if the diminution of cholera, in the districts partly supplied with the improved water, depended on this supply, the houses receiving it would be the houses enjoying the whole benefit of the diminution of the malady, whilst the houses supplied with the water from Battersea-fields would suffer the same mortality as they would if the improved supply did not exist at all. As there is no difference whatever, either in the houses or in the people receiving the supply of the two water companies, or in any of the physical conditions with which they are surrounded, it is obvious that no experiment could have been devised which would more thoroughly test the effect of water-supply on the progress of cholera than this, which circumstances placed ready-made before the observer."

The inquiry gave striking results. In the first seven weeks of the epidemics, the proportion of deaths to 10,000 houses, was, in those supplied by the Southwark and Vauxhall Company, 315; while in those supplied by the Lambeth Company, it was but 37. In the second seven weeks, when other means of communication came into operation, the difference was not quite so great; but even then the population supplied by the Southwark and Vauxhall continued to suffer nearly five times the mortality of that supplied by the Lambeth!

And this leads us to speak, though briefly, of the state of the Thames. Last summer its condition was found to be frightful. It is so still; and when the hot weather arrives, this will be evident. It is to be hoped no one drinks of it. If any do, we would shout with Buckstone, in "The Unequal Match,"—"Rash man, forbear!—it's *beastly!*" For years past the deterioration of the river has been noticed; and from time to time endeavours have been made to direct attention to the subject as one of great public interest. Every day increases the evil. Without taking into consideration the immense annual growth of London, it must be borne in mind that other large districts give their refuse to the river. There are also gas-works, most unwholesome manufactories, slaughter-houses, cow-sheds, stables, breweries, and the drainage of thickly-filled graveyards, to aid the mischief; and yet intelligent men can be found to maintain the *salubrity of the Thames*. The health of thousands must be affected by it, and what *may* occur cannot be calmly contemplated.

Whilst examining in the summer the north shore of the Thames from the Houses of Parliament to London-bridge (a most unpleasant task), we made a rough measurement at about the time of low water, and are disposed to think that there is an average breadth of 100 feet of the most putrid soil skirting this edge of our great city for some hours during each day. We were told by several persons who are employed in this neighbourhood, that in parts the deposit is more than six feet deep: the whole of this is thickly impregnated with impure matter, and at the opening of such sewers as have not been passed into the river beyond low-water mark, the condition is too bad for description.

Many of our readers may have noticed the black, offensive, and dangerous matter which is taken from choked drains in the neighbourhood of cesspools. There are many thousands of tons of equally poisonous stuff on the shore of the Thames. A considerable quantity of such matter is kept in solution by the action of the tide and the steam-vessels, which adds materially to the bad state of the water.

While wandering along this putrid shore, which is both a shame and a wonder in the nineteenth century, thoughts arise, in spite of some overpowering feelings, of other days, of processions of stately barges, full of the influential citizens in whose hands the protection of Father Thames was placed. This body found the stream clean and wholesome; the apprentices and citizens came from long distances to avail themselves of the water-supply. For years festive bands of citizens, at stated intervals, mingling pleasure with business, went forth to survey the important charge, which was in a healthy condition, intrusted to their care: now Father Thames has become such a castaway that the Lord Mayor has declared that he cannot again venture on a visit. The days of "swan-hopping" and river perambulation are at an end.

One Sunday evening last summer, just after low water, we passed along the shore. And all who would have an idea of the extent to which the Thames is used, should visit the landing-place at Hungerford-bridge on a fine Sunday evening. The day had been cooler than some days previously; nevertheless, the stench at different points was frightful, and produced a sickness which lasted till the next morning. Bad as was the state of affairs at the time referred to, the watermen at the landing-places said the air was "lavender" to what it had been. Early in the morning, they continued, when the first steam-packets begin to move about, the smell is enough to strike down strong men. During a few hours of the night, when there is but little traffic, the heavy matter sinks, and the renewed agitation in the morning causes the escape of pungent gases, of a most poisonous description. Even the dipping of the oars, at early hours, produces a sickening sensation. The weight of the impure portion of Thames water is a peculiarity which formerly caused the water to be held in much favour by sailors for long foreign voyages. Large establishments were formed for the purpose of filtering it ; but even so lately as 1840 and 1841, many ships took it without this process from the outside of the docks. A person who has sailed from the Thames, but who is now a waterman, described how that he had been twelve months and upwards on board ship with Thames water, obtained in the manner just mentioned, and that it remained good all the time : the heavy earthy matters settled firmly to the bottom of the casks ; but on the bung being started, it was necessary to give the water " a wide berth," for the smell was almost unbearable—sometimes the force of the gas had burst out the bungs with a report like that of a pistol. A similar process, on a large scale, is going on daily on the Thames. The soil, put in motion by the action of the water, is now more considerable than formerly ; and the amount of poisonous gases which is thrown off is proportionate to the increase of the sewage which is passed into the stream. Fifteen or sixteen years ago the Thames water was not so bad, and persons on the river did not hesitate at dipping in a vessel and drinking the contents. Such a thing now would be like an act of insanity ; and yet we are told, on good authority, that in a part of Rotherhithe a number of poor persons, who have no proper water-supply, are obliged to use, for drinking and other purposes, the Thames water in its present abominable condition, unfiltered. This is a matter which should receive immediate attention.

In order to form a proper notion of the condition of the Thames shore, it is necessary not to restrict the examination to the landing-places alone—for care is taken at these points to remove the slimy matter as much as possible ;—but even here, as we found at one place by an excavation, there is a depth of more than four feet of poisonous soil ; and it is certain that a large portion of this is cesspool refuse.

In considering the effect of the condition of the Thames on the health of the metropolis, it must be borne in mind that the actual number of those who dwell on the shore is small in comparison with those who merely remain all day in the neighbourhood. Thousands are employed during the day only, in the docks, the canals, and in the large manufactories, warehouses, and other establishments which line the river ; most of these workmen travel long distances to closer neighbourhoods after the labours of the day are ended, so that there may be a difficulty in clearly tracing the amount of mischief which is actually caused by the pestilential condition of the Thames. The docks especially are a fertile source of disease.

When in this district, we glanced at the basin and other parts of the Regent's Canal, and found that a large quantity of water is daily passed from this important work into the river. The water was very cloudy, and of a brownish colour ; but, compared with that

of the Thames, its purity looked remarkable, and there is not a large
amount of animal refuse in this tributary. Complaints are, however,
made of certain offensive manufactures which drain into one of the

The Wedding of the Waters at the Regent's Canal.

branches. "But, in order to show you that we do good rather than
harm," said a superintendent on duty, "please to look here, where
the Thames is just beginning to flow into the entrance-lock of the

canal." And truly the effect was a startling one. The stream of the Thames, of a sable hue, "thick and slab," could be seen meeting and invading the canal, presenting such an appearance as might be expected by the bursting close by of several hogsheads of Warren's

Life in a Cesspool.

blacking,—a much more obvious and less gratifying difference, we need not say, than is observable where the Rhine meets the Moselle.

> " Like the two lives that are blended
>   When the loneliness is ended,
> The loneliness each heart hath known so well ;
>   Like the sun and moon together,
>   In a sky of splendid weather,
> Is the marriage of the Rhine and the Moselle,"—

writes Mr. Arnold ; and although it will not apply to the marriage of the Thames and the Regent's Canal, it will serve to sweeten a dirty subject. The sketch (p. 54) does not exaggerate the contrast. The sides and bottoms of boats become covered with solid matter; objects are not visible at even an inch below the surface; the reflection of ships is very faint, but shadows almost as strong as those on land are thrown on the face of the water by the sunshine. When gravely pondering these things, De Foe's description of the neglected condition of London at the time of the visit of the Great Plague of 1665 comes to mind; and we think, with Byron, of "ships rotting, sailorless," and other uncomfortable associations.

In passing along the foul shore, we came to one of the Thames tributaries, and the scene so clearly illustrates an existing evil, that we have drawn it for the benefit of the public (p. 55). This place is a creek which extends some distance inland, similar to that which has been so much complained of near Blackfriars-bridge. At the north end is a large sewer, which drains Bow-common, and all buildings in that direction. The mouth is partly covered by a loose iron flap, which, when the tide is out, allows the sewage-water to flow in a rapid stream. Dwelling-houses are built on the sewer wall, and around it. The people living about here have, in most instances, sickly children, who in a measure resemble the poor plants observable in some of the windows about. Everything around is bad. The bank, when the tide goes out, is covered with filth; and when the number of the similar tributaries which flow to Father Thames, both night and day, is recollected, his state is not to be wondered at.

Both Houses of Parliament were loud last session in their condemnation of the existing state of things. They have the evil at their own door—a retribution,—for it is certain that the present conditions are in a great measure the result of want of forethought and consideration of the subject. And let our provincial cities and towns take warning in time, and avoid the transformation of their rivers into reeking sewers and decomposing cess-banks, which act upon health, and degrade character.

During the discussion of the mode to be adopted in draining London, the assertion that sewage-matter is washed backwards and forwards by the tide, and is long before it gets out to sea, was derided. The fact, however, is unquestionable. Look at the next sketch. It shows the way in which a dead dog, under our own eyes, travelled. We thought he would get away: however, after a time, and after whirling and resting amongst the posts and barges, the dead dog came again in sight, moving *against the tide*, but much nearer to the shore; he turns off again towards the sea, and returns this time much sooner than the last; and after describing various circles, as shown by the arrows in the sketch, he is deposited in the slime, together with other specimens of his own and allied families.

An artist living on the banks of the Thames, near Lambeth, says, "I like to look out at the beautiful river, for in an artist's eye it is still beautiful at many times of the day, and often my pleasure has been marred by dogs and cats : I have seen a dog one morning floating past—he has come back again with the next tide, and for

A Dog in the Thames.

several days I had only to look at my clock in order to know the position of my visitor ; he was larger each visit, and at last disappeared."

CHAPTER X.

As we are on the Thames, let us look at a swamp which is called a town—Canning-town,—unknown to the great mass of Londoners.

We all know the consequences of planting large populations on ill-adapted lands, without making provision for that most important necessary of accumulated life, *drainage;* and it might have been hoped that the sad effects in known instances would have led to the prevention of other similar mistakes. It is, however, not so ; for in the Plaistow Marshes, Canning-town has been commenced, without the provision of either proper roads or drainage.

On one side of the new town an earthen embankment dams off the water of the Bow Creek. The level on which all the houses are placed is below that of the ordinary half-height of the Thames. Standing near the iron bridge which crosses Bow Creek, let us take a peep at the scene which presents itself. Near at hand is the new town, and on all sides of the green level London is marching with giant strides. A few years since, if a dozen people were seen crossing this bridge in the course of a day, it was a matter of wonder : now the bridge has become a great thoroughfare. Nine or ten years since there were only two or three houses, and now look at the number of them !

In the view of Canning-town, as it appears from near to the iron bridge, the green level is shown spreading over a great extent. Along the margin of this flat land, in every direction, houses, shops, public-houses, and churches, are to be seen skirting the level, and gaining every week further and further upon the space, which is chiefly *several feet below the high-water mark of the Thames.* The new town, which already consists of several long streets, will, in the course of a few years, spread out and meet the approaching houses, and all this level will be planted with dwellings and inhabited by many thousands of people. The artificial bank of Bow Creek and the embankment of the Thames are all that prevent the houses here from being flooded every high tide. To provide for the effectual drainage of this district, by the ordinary means, is impossible. The houses here have been erected without the means of either carrying off the refuse or properly avoiding damp. In course of time the *débris* of these and other houses will raise the level; but in the mean time what will be the sacrifice of human life which must take place without prompt measures. With some difficulty we managed to reach the place on foot from the turnpike road, and found the condition of the streets miserable : many of them, although the day was tolerably fine, were almost impassable, and vehicles sank nearly up to the axletrees in the mud. In many parts were great pools of stagnant water. At the beginning of 1856 the writer said,—" If something is not done, in two or three years' time the ground will be poisoned by cesspools, water will stand on the surface, and evils of a serious nature will follow. In a score of years or less, Canning-town will be an important place, with its churches, omnibus and cab stations, and its masses of rich and poor. Let us hope for the introduction of measures proportionate to the extent of the future requirements. Flesh and blood are precious materials."

In 1857 an outbreak of cholera proved the truth of the prediction, and great efforts were made to obtain improvements in the drainage of the place, and such other mitigations of its miserable condition as might render the development of disease less likely. The President of the Board, the Right Hon. Mr. Cowper, went down immediately, and found houses without drainage, without ventilation, without water-supply, except of the worst description, ditches presenting an evaporating surface of the foulest kind, and the roads a mass of mud and filth ; the whole being a marsh seven feet below high-water mark. In Vicarage-terrace the only drain available is a sink *under the pump, into which they habitually empty all the slops of their houses!* The sink communicates with the well, and the people have no other water to drink ! The Board addressed the Local Board of Health, calling upon them to take "immediate and effective measures for removing, or at least for mitigating," conditions so conducive to the development of the disease, under which most of the inhabitants of their districts are placed; and a system of drainage is to be carried out." The erection of dwelling-places in such a position should not

BOW CREEK

J. B.

Canning-Town : a hybrid Suburb.

have been permitted. Being here, their owners must do what can be done to save life. Flesh and blood, as we before said, *are* precious materials, and the country cannot afford to indulge in preventable disease, involuntary demoralization, and premature deaths.

The cesspool system is fraught with danger, and must on no account be permitted. In some of the old neighbourhoods it is not possible to discover whether there are cesspools or not, the disguise being artfully managed; though the arrangement is such as to throw deadly emanations into the house. A few months ago, the cesspool of a house in Islington was disguised; and it is worth while to record the following circumstances connected with it.

The cesspool, serving for three houses, had been covered over and trapped : of course, it was speedily filled with liquid, which became daily more impure, and was passed to the imperfect drain, and to the untrapped sinks. Moreover, the whole basement of the house was impregnated with impure matter. The upper part of this house (three rooms) was occupied by a family of eight persons (six children—the wife was soon after arrival confined). At the time of removal to this place, a more healthy-looking group of children could not be found : soon after moving hither from a more northern part of Islington, where the drainage was complete, the complexion of the children became daily more pallid. It was difficult, notwithstanding all endeavours, to get ventilation at night, or to rise in the morning, in consequence of a drowsiness. In a few weeks the children were more or less troubled with eruptions of the skin. Soon after, four of them were attacked with measles—in two instances followed by hooping-cough, and in another by low fever. After the confinement of the wife, she was placed in great danger, and exhibited symptoms that were not likely to occur in a well-drained and properly-ventilated dwelling. The infant, from its birth, had a cough that seriously affected its chest. The eldest child failed in health, and was, eventually, seized with rheumatic fever. It should be mentioned, that this ill-conditioned habitation was situated in rather a low position, not far from the Regent's Canal : this, no doubt, added to the evil. The change in the children, in the short space of about two months, was remarkable, and was a practical and clear illustration of the want of sanitary arrangements. Besides the ill-health above mentioned, a young man, living in the lower part of the premises, had a very serious attack of typhus fever about the time the infant and another child were suffering from bronchitis,which rapidly ended fatally in the case of the former. We will not maintain that this might not have happened in other circumstances. Only six or seven weeks elapsed after the removal of this family to a healthy locality, before the improvement in their condition was as remarkable as its change for worse was on the other occasion. An example like this may have more weight than a volume of precepts.

Medals are given very properly by the Humane Society for saving lives from fire and water ; might it not be wise to give honour to those who, by the aid of knowledge, prevent death ? In the small city of Ely, by the aid of sanitary science, upwards of seventy-two lives are saved in each year. It is terrible to think of the multitudes who die annually from preventable causes in large towns.

CHAPTER XI.

AN esteemed friend, who commands a poetic pen as well as a feeling heart, wrote us not long ago, on the condition of dwellers in a rural location, and seemed to feel it as rather surprising, if the statement were correct as to the value of pure air, that men and women and children fall victims to disease, and are constantly cut off prematurely, even *in the country.* " I went out last evening," says the writer, living in a retired part of a most healthful county, "mounted the high ground, and sat me down to see the sunset, to listen to the talk of the swans and the chatter of the frogs, and to hear the village church clock strike nine ! It was such an evening ; so even then, I could not go home, but watched one star appear, and the night-hawks come swooping down on to—I suppose, a poor little frog, that had been croaking quite musically close beside me. Its song was suddenly stilled, and the hawks flew off, clapping their wings noisily, and I strolled homewards, counting the glow-worms by the way." The writer goes on to describe the out-of-health condition of some cottiers who were visited on the road, and says the question then occurred to which we have already given expression. Now, so far from its being surprising that dwellers in some of the rural districts have unnecessary illness, and die before their time, it seems extraordinary in many cases that they escape so well, when we know the effect of decomposing vegetable matter, stagnant horseponds, reeking ditches, ill-drained and undrained cow-sheds and stables. Locations which look perfectly healthy are often, through human mismanagement, mere pest-holes. Over-leaf is a sketch of a village on the Welsh borders, near Shrewsbury, as seen from a distance ;—pleasantly placed, blown on by the pure fresh air, and a charming object to the passing tourist. "Innocence and Health must be dwellers there," says the passer-by. He begins to inquire, however, and he finds, to say nothing about Innocence, that Health, at any rate, is a stranger ; fever is a constant guest. The second sketch shows some of the cottages when you are amongst them. The place is without drainage. Pigs and dogs are kept : the people are dirty in their habits, and allow all kinds of refuse to collect : water flows down the hill, and lodges in pools, which become stagnant ; and the consequence is, that in this position, which would be perfectly healthy if effectually drained, fever is, as we have said, a frequent visitor. If the statistics of such neighbourhoods were given, the results would startle the most careless thinkers.

The first sanitary requirement is thorough drainage. When placing good drainage in the first place, we do not do so without considering the evil which is constantly arising from the unwholesomeness of some wells, through the filtering of various kinds of refuse into the springs.

A Fever Village near Shrewsbury, from a Distance.

"Who would think it?"

Part of the same Village, close.

"Who would doubt it?"

Good paving is very desirable; for if this be not attended to, even with great care, the waste water sinks into the earth, which in time becomes a mass of putrid soil, and this in the summer time is attended with ill effects. One of our sketches shows how the well (with the luxury of a pump), to which many of the neighbours come for water, is situated. It adjoins a cesspool: the adjacent soil is saturated with the impurities of many years, and the nearest doctor has more patients than pay. Sometimes, too, we have found the water-tank close under the wall of the village graveyard !

When all has been done that drainage can effect, it is necessary to bear carefully in mind the effect produced on the mouse in the closed jar, and the Englishmen in the Black-hole of Calcutta; for if we have a room or a house filled with even healthful atmosphere, it will soon be spoiled and rendered unwholesome if the air be not renewed. Look into the bedrooms of some of the cottages, and you will find them

A Bedroom in a State of Insalubrity.

"Poisonous Air."

The Position of the Pump.

"Poisonous Water."

overcrowded to a most dangerous extent;—the man and his wife and five or six children, of all ages, sleeping in one apartment, in order to let the little room at the back to three or four farm labourers, or, when a railway is going on, to half a dozen navvies. In the first place, there must be, as we have already said, a certain cubical area in a room for each person that is to occupy it, and then there should be the means of ventilating this area—renewing the air. In the majority of even good dwellings the arrangements for this are most insufficient. Our sketch, which represents the best bedroom in the best inn of the neighbourhood, will give an idea of the condition to which the greater number of bedrooms are reduced by the morning. The air is tolerably pure as high as the mantel-piece, supposing there *be* a fire-place in it, and above that, the foul air is incompetent to maintain healthful life ;—and not merely that—not merely deprived of its life-sustaining principle, but impregnated with a death-giver,—foul gases and the emanations from decomposition.

But how can the atmosphere—invisible, tasteless—convey these impurities? it has been asked. In the ordinary light which exists between the brightest sunshine and darkness, the atmosphere seems, so far as appearance goes, pure and harmless. When the sun shines, however, through narrow channels, into this seeming void, the motes in the sunbeam show that the atmosphere is anything but transparent : countless myriads of minute atoms of matter are constantly floating in the atmosphere, and entering the lungs of young and old. Here then is palpable evidence of the necessity for care. The semi-opaque nature of the air we breathe, is evident ; and far smaller particles, which the eye cannot see, are constantly rising from the surface and floating around,—germs of disease, emissaries of death.

In ill-paved streets, and back yards in a similar condition, on which waste water is allowed to remain and saturate the soil, when the drainage from cesspools also further pollutes the earth, exhalations fill the air, and poison the system of those who are unfortunately obliged to inhale this important necessary of life so adulterated. Those who, in the cleanest and best-ventilated houses of the metropolis, have noticed the thick layer of dust that in one day covers tables, books, and the surface of every other object, can form an idea of the large quantity of these floating atoms which enters the mouth, both during day and night, at every respiration.

If the dust on the walls and floor of a room in which tobacco has been smoked be swept up, and then carefully packed away, on examination, after some time, it will be found that the tobacco fumes are still detectable. Window hangings, carpets, and other fabrics, will absorb the gases thrown off by tobacco, sulphur, and similar matter. In the same way the bad gases arising from overcrowded sleeping-rooms, or drains, pervade and lodge themselves to a considerable extent on all surrounding objects, and poison those motes made evident to us by the sunbeam; and which, even when the bright sunlight does not make them visible, are still surely performing the never-ceasing work. Although in ships at sea, on mountain-tops, on moors and marshes, the motes, showing the never-ceasing operations of nature, glisten in the sunshine, there is a difference between the wholesomeness of such dust and that which arises in the houses of polluted courts, in the neighbourhood of crowded graveyards, in ill-ventilated assembly-rooms, overcrowded barracks, and other places. The particles of dust loaded with fever and contagion are readily borne upon the breeze from ill-conditioned and hidden places to those adjoining, and, of course, to a certain extent adulterate the better atmosphere.

As an instance of the extent to which scents can be borne, it may be mentioned that when the wind has been blowing gently in the right direction, we have often distinctly identified, in Holborn and in parts of the City, the pleasant smell of the new hay from the meadows on the north of London. In like manner dangerous nuisances are floated on the air ; and this circumstance, together with the sight of the motes in the sunbeam, ought to be a lesson to us that large masses of the poor cannot be neglected with impunity, and should teach us that it is necessary to preserve the atmosphere from pollution. It is a ready medium for subtler matters than those we have been pointing to, whether in the country or the town.

It has been said that good health is a mark of respectability, and so it is ; and, moreover, it shows good sense,—for it is not merely an evidence usually that vicious dissipation has been avoided, but that the laws of nature have been understood and attended to.

CHAPTER XII.

NOTHING interferes more with the improvement of the masses of the people than the difficulty there is of getting rid of old customs ; for instance, the practice of keeping the dead before inter-ment for a week or more, so hard to break down, has, in many instances, been the means of destroying the health and lives of the living. For many years infants were " swaddled " in the remarkable manner shown in old manuscripts and pictures. It would be as difficult to form an estimate of the number who have been killed by such processes as of the girls who have died prematurely from the effects of tight-lacing. At one time, in cases of small-pox and similar diseases, every breath of air was carefully excluded, as though that life-preserving element were an enemy instead of a friend. When this treatment was in fashion, the small-pox was about as fatal as the cholera is when it visits us. Fever patients used to be closed up in a similar manner, and the beds of the sufferers were piled with blankets.

These errors, and fifty more, have been, to a considerable extent, lessened. There are, however, a large number of persons amongst the less educated with whom the fashion of former days is still considered the best, in spite of its evident ill effects. Many an intelligent artisan and his wife who would laugh at most of the practices alluded to, would decline availing themselves of a home, however wholesome, which did not present the appearance of those built upon the old plan. Thousands who feel the difficulty prefer the fashion, and with their families live in subdivided houses, where, in many instances, the benefits of privacy, cleanliness, and comfort cannot exist, in preference to occupying dwellings which, although different in outward form, have the means of family seclusion, and all the necessaries for health. It is a pity that it should be so; but such being the case, it is necessary to use means which, while being beneficial, will humour the prejudiced taste that exists; and credit is due to those who devise proper means of coaxing the great industrious multitude into the use of the kind of houses which are so much required. We have more than once suggested in these pages, how desirable it is to provide houses at a moderate rent that would afford the advantages of separate residences and other necessary qualities, and would as nearly as possible present the appearance of the dwellings now in use.

We have found in one of the northern towns this principle carried out to a considerable extent in some of the new streets. The houses towards the road present a substantial-looking front, two stories high from the pavement, with rooms below looking into a very wide area. In the front of each house are two doors, fitted with knockers; one of these, by means of *a distinct passage*, leads to the ground-floor, and the other to the floor above, while a railed flight of steps affords entrance to the apartments below. We have thus in each house three distinct sets of rooms. The back is furnished with galleries, something in the same manner as the model cottage which was erected by Prince Albert near the Great Exhibition, with staircases leading to the back premises. The upper and the ground floor of those houses, which consist of three rooms each, let for £10 a year each (less than 4s. a week), including taxes; the places below for less: and we were told that they are occupied as quickly as they can be finished, by respectable workmen, and that they pay about 8 per cent.

Every single step of this kind is encouraging, and it is unnecessary to deny that many such have been taken. Notwithstanding the enormous extent of the ignorance yet prevailing, and the amount of work required to be done, all parts of the country show the gradual admittance of the truth of those principles from which improvement must result. Twenty years ago, the great mass of even the middle and well-informed classes were not aware of the dangers with which they were beset. Glance back to former times, and it seems remarkable how people lived at all. Take, for instance, many country villages. The houses were chiefly planted in the form of a street, in the centre of which were two rows of " midden-steads " and pigsties: stagnant pools of the foulest description were collected in all directions, and the stale garbage and other refuse were left in small mountains in all seasons: there were of course cesspools in the rear, for no attempt at proper drainage had been made. And bad as this was, the condition of the towns was worse. We recollect seeing in an important town a large churchyard raised to the height of not less than twelve feet above the proper surface by the mouldering dead. It was managed in a way which would perhaps have surprised even the workers in Spa-fields and some metropolitan grounds. People even then used to wonder how room could be made for more tenants. But there was no George Alfred Walker to look in and investigate their " doings." * It was by no means unusual to drain this ground without disguise, and let it run along the public street to the nearest gully-hole. If one had at that time lifted up his voice against such a practice, he would have been thought fit for a place in the neighbouring lunatic asylum. Lanes thickly surrounded this graveyard, and one narrow turning led to a series of little squares and back nooks. There was no drainage in any part, and yet perhaps not less than 200 or 300 persons inhabited the houses which were reached by the narrow archway. There was also a long building used as a school, where nearly 200 children were constantly assembled. In front of the school was a place for all the refuse. Behind was a closet, with cesspool, which was constantly overflowing, and which was the only convenience for the boys, and for a large number of the inhabitants. At times the huge dirt-heap would be removed, and the task would occupy two or three days.

When cholera broke out in the town for the first time, not a single house in this court escaped ; in some instances whole families were swept away. Then the houses in these confined places were not supplied with water ; people had none except such as they could catch from the drip of the roofs in rainy weather, or carry from the nearest pump or conduit ; while total want of drainage and the accumulation of putrid refuse, caused an atmosphere indescribably close and oppressive.

It is of the utmost consequence that a knowledge of the laws which govern human life should be given to women. A frightful loss of infant life occurs through their want of this knowledge. In a certain unhealthy district of London during one year, forty-four deaths occurred, and of these twenty-six who died were children under five years of age. The difference in the proportion of deaths amongst infants in various localities shows that this loss is unnecessary. Thousands of preventable deaths which occur, both in London and the provinces, from other than sanitary imperfections, are clearly to be traced to the ignorance of the mothers in the simplest principles of healthful management. In the National and other schools in which the future mothers of the next race of English workmen are being educated, attention should be given to the instruction of the young, not only in sanitary matters, but as to the structure and functions of the body. To the mothers we have to look for the education of the world. " When shall I begin the education of my child," said a young woman once to a wise man ; " it is now four years old ? " " Madam," he replied, " you have lost three years already. From the first smile that gleams over an infant's cheek, your opportunity begins."

In nine cases out of ten, amongst the poorer classes, intemperate mothers are ignorant that by their course of life they either poison their infants, or, at any rate, weaken their systems. If the common

* The neglect which Mr. Walker has experienced is not creditable to his contemporaries. He has his reward, however, in the success which crowned his labours.

and useful knowledge to which we allude were made a more important consideration, some might thereby be prevented from committing what they would know to be acts of wickedness. Quite true it is, that "in exalting the faculties of the soul, we annihilate, in a great degree, the delusion of the senses."

"Murder done here!" should be written up in many districts of England. Of the people who live in Eastbourne, Sussex, fifteen of every 1,000 die during the year. Of the people who live in Liverpool, thirty-six of every 1,000 die in the same time. And, to take two places that are closer together : while of every 1,000 persons in Kensington nineteen die every year ; of those who live in St. Saviour's, Southwark, thirty-three of every 1,000 die in the same period. And we know why. And much of the evil could be prevented, and it is not. Surely, then, we should not be going beyond the truth in writing up in that parish, "Murder done here !"

Reports of the Registrar-General show that at least one-fourth of the annual mortality of England is of artificial production, and that of the 628 registration districts, in sixty-four (containing a population of about 1,000,000 inhabitants), the death-rate ranges from 1,500 to 1,700 in each 100,000 ; but the average death-rate of all England is about 2,266 ; and nearly nine-tenths of the registration districts of England show death-rates that are in excess of 1,700, and which, in some notorious cases, run up to 3,100, 3,300, and 3,600, the latter being an excess of deaths over the most healthy districts of 2,100 in the 100,000.

Death by old age is, physiologically speaking, the only normal death of men. There are, however, differences of longevity ; some men are so constitutionally weak, that they virtually die of old age before their sixtieth year ; but it cannot, says Mr. Simon, " be far from the truth to assume that were there no artificial interference with the duration of life, death by natural decay would, in this country, under its present circumstances, usually happen about eighty years of age." In the Faro Islands, with a population of 8,000, the period for death by old age is between eighty and ninety years. But this physiological fact must be guarded from misapplication ; for an amount of premature deaths is a certainty, quite irrespective of the immediate influence of exterior circumstances.

Families in which gout, rheumatism, tubercular, and other diseases are hereditary, have not the average expectation of healthy life, and a certain share of every generation has in it from these sources the seeds of premature death. It is to be noted, however, that even under the worst of these circumstances, much good is effected by properly-directed efforts.

The average number of those deaths which, in the present condition of society, must be considered as not preventable, may be gathered from the equality of deaths from peculiar complaints in all the districts of England.

If all men lived to their full term of eighty years, the death-rates in 100,000 would be 1,250 ; and experience seems to show that there are populations in which there are only 1,500, 1,600, and 1,700 deaths per annum in the 100,000, and that a million of the inhabitants of England are living in these comparatively favourable districts ; and fixing, then, 1,250 as the theoretical standard of right deaths, we find that in the best circumstances in England, 250, 350, and 450 extra deaths in every thousand are to be attributed to diseases—some, it is true, not now preventable—which have caused premature death.

That some districts of England are greatly more fatal than others, affords strong *primâ facie* grounds for believing that the local excesses of mortality are due to local circumstances of aggravation, and that these aggravating local circumstances are such as it is possible to counteract ; and that, consequently, of the total mortality ascribed to these influences in England, a very large share is preventable.

" Thousands of deaths annually arise from such diseases as are in the most absolute sense preventable,—diseases which either will not arise, or will not spread, in communities which follow certain well-known sanitary laws. For, first, there are certain diseases, of which it is hardly a metaphor to say, that they consist in the extension of a putrefactive process from matters outside the body to matters inside the body,—diseases of which the very essence is filth,—diseases which have no local habitation except where putrefiable air or putrefiable water furnishes means for their rise or propagation,—diseases against which there may be found a complete security in the cultivation of public and private cleanliness. Yet some tens of thousands of deaths annually arise in England from these diseases ! "

Surely, then, we may write up, " Murder done here ! "

And again, there are diseases of other kinds, which annually kill some thousands more of our population, though the appointed preventives are so definite and so accessible that scarcely a death from such causes ought to occur in any civilized country. The preventable diseases, cholera, diarrhœa, and dysentery, during nine years,—1848-56,—have been fatal to 237,498 persons. In two years (1849 and 1854), when cholera was epidemic, there died from the above causes 116,248 persons. (If in warfare such a multitude should meet their death, it would be considered a dire calamity.) A large proportion of the excess of deaths in those years occurred during a few summer weeks, when the epidemic influence was at its height.

It is truly remarked, that if a single felon were known to die in England at the present day under circumstances which eighty-five years ago were the rule and habit of prison life, the whole strength of public opinion would express itself as against a murder. Yet outside the privileged area, fever continues its ravages. 17,000 or 18,000 victims of fever are annually slain,—the chief part from our labouring population,—and many more are laid prostrate by this cause for weeks and months, their families impoverished, and often brought to ruin and pauperism.

Howard closed his memorable appeal by suggesting that " if no

mercy be due to prisoners, the gaol distemper is a national concern
of no small importance."

"Its claims to this rank of importance are surely not yet at an
end, while its causes remain virulent in the houses of our working
population, while its cruel contagion is maintained at their cost, and
while so many thousand lives are yearly sacrificed to the negligence
which lets it continue."

CHAPTER XIII.

WE have classed hospitals and dispensaries amongst our Social
Bridges; and so they should be. But we must not include hospitals
that kill more than they cure; and this is the case with many
throughout the kingdom. Hospitals, beyond any other buildings,
demand the most careful arrangements—not merely for the ample
supply of air, but to insure that the air so supplied be *pure*. So
little has this been attended to in days gone by, that there are many
hospitals in this country where, as soon as the wards get full, fevers
and other disorders appear, and it is difficult to effect a cure in many
cases which, under other circumstances, would be overcome without
difficulty. A leading Edinburgh professor, in some recently published
" Memoirs," says,—" I have often stated and taught that, if our
present medical, surgical, and obstetric hospitals were changed, from
being crowded palaces with a layer of sick in each flat, into villages
or cottages with one, or at most two, patients in each room, a great
saving of human life would be effected. And if the village were
constructed of iron (as is now sometimes done for other purposes),
instead of brick or stone, it could be taken down and rebuilt every
few years; a matter, apparently, of much moment in hospital hygiene.
Besides, the value of the material would not greatly deteriorate from
use : the principal outlay would be in the first cost of it. It could
be erected in any vacant space or spaces of ground, within or around
a city, that chanced to be unoccupied ; and, in cases of epidemics, the
accommodation could always be at once and readily increased."

There is value in the hint, but it is only in exceptional cases that
it could be resorted to. Hospitals must still be erected, and we
must take care that every available means be used to render them
healthful and fit for their purpose. Some of our military hospitals
are disgraceful to the scientific character of the country; and it never
fell to our lot to visit any in which there were not obvious errors
that might have been avoided. With respect to the vital importance
of fresh air for the maintenance of life, it would really seem as if the
world were not to be convinced on this head : you may remind them
of the Black-hole-of-Calcutta story ; of the canary-bird that dies in
a night hung up under your bed-curtains ; or of the 250 Coolies who,
in a few hours, were killed a year or so ago in an American vessel,

by having been forced under hatches. It is all of no use : the facts are assented to : the necessity of plenty of air is fully admitted ; and then, on the very first occasion, the assenters proceed to act as if they had never heard of such a necessity, or did not believe in it if they had.

We have long fought for fresh air,—fresh air everywhere. What we would now more especially speak of is the arrangement of hospitals for the sick and wounded,—a subject the more urgent because of the large sums about to be spent in the provision of additional structures of that kind.

Mr. John Roberton, of Manchester, rightly points out that in constructing hospitals we have been in the habit of confounding together two things widely different; namely, *sick wards and dormitories ;* wards, where the sick and wounded lie continuously throughout the day and night, with dormitories occupied by the healthy for only eight or nine hours in the twenty-four ;—of confounding wards —where cubic air space, though highly important, is a secondary consideration to the getting rid of fœtid and pestiferous exhalations by a continual renewal of the atmosphere—with dormitories, in which ample cubic air space is all that is required. " It has been owing to ignorance or inattention to this essential difference between wards for the sick and dormitories for the healthy, that we have few hospitals in England that are not insalubrious whenever they chance to be crowded ; and which, when crowded with such cases as burns, compound fractures, and extensive ulcers, are often the abodes of death, occurring in forms most humbling and mortifying to the pride of surgical science ; since the surgeon, in such circumstances, is aware that the poor sufferers have been carried to a public institution to their destruction ; and that, had they been treated by him in their own homes, howsoever humble these might be, the chances of recovery would have been greater."

The prime defect in the great majority of our hospitals is, that of their being constructed after the plan of an hotel, well suited to have lodged persons in a state of health, but incapable of the proper degree of ventilation when crowded with sick, especially those of a surgical class. There is, moreover, another evil attaching to this plan of building, distinct from the other,—the creation of what is justly denominated *an hospital atmosphere,* which arises from the wards communicating with one another by passages and stairs. It is owing to this kind of intercommunication that, if a foul state of the air happen in only a single ward, such foul air spreads and speedily pollutes the entire building.

The principles carried out in the arrangement of French hospitals were laid down seventy years ago, after long investigation, by a number of skilful medical men in France, so as best to unite health and convenience in such an edifice. " One of the conditions," says Mr. Gwilt, " prescribed by their programme, was the complete insulation of each apartment, as well as an easy communication by covered galleries round the building, and these were required to be of such extended dimensions, that the air around should be unobstructed and circulating in every part with freedom ; thus affording a wholesome promenade for the patients." Durand, in his *Parallèle d'Edifices,* gives the plans of many of the finest hospitals in Europe, and amongst them the plan of the Hospital de la Roquette, the designs for which were made by Poyet, about 1788, on the instructions referred to. "In this design each room, as well those on one side of the establishment for the males, as those on the other side for the females, is appropriated to one particular disease. Each of these rooms is about thirty-two feet wide and thirty feet six inches high. Behind the beds (which are in two rows in each room) runs a passage, about three feet four inches wide, which removes them so much from the walls, and allows, therefore, of the necessary waiting on the invalids, and hides the wardrobe attached to each bed in the window recesses. Above these passages, which are about six feet six inches high, is arranged on each side a row of windows, by which ventilation as well as light is obtained."

When the plan of the Victoria Military Hospital, now in course of erection near Southampton, was first made known, the writer found himself compelled to object to the arrangements, and said that should the proposed arrangement be carried out, whenever this hospital should be full of patients, more disease would be generated there than cured. It was scoffed at at the time, but the truth of it became more and more evident : alterations have been made, but whether or not to a sufficient extent remains to be seen.

There are hospitals on very bad sites : there are hospitals on comparatively good sites ; but there is hardly an instance, in this country at least, of both hospital and site fully embodying those sanitary principles which are essentially necessary for the rapid recovery of the sick and maimed.

Air of sufficient purity is not to be obtained in towns. Every existing town hospital ought therefore to be removed into the country, if it be possible to do so. At a moderate distance from towns land is much cheaper than in close-built places ; and there are many large hospital establishments covering considerable areas of ground in crowded and valuable parts of towns and cities, which might be removed to the country not only with incalculable advantage to the sick, but with great pecuniary gain to the hospital establishment. Even in so vast a place as the metropolis, a few casualty wards, where accidents might temporarily be seen, rooms for the examination and the reception of cases, and suitable vehicles for transferring them to the country, would be all that would be necessary to effect the reform.

The fundamental idea of all hospital plans ought to be this : to have pure fresh air in every part of the building. Fresh air is the *sine quâ non.* Unless a building can be so planned that the sick shall breathe air as fresh within its walls as they could do externally, they will suffer in a ratio corresponding to the degree of impurity.

Let any one conversant with the phenomena of disease go into a badly-constructed, and, consequently, ill-ventilated ward, and look at the sick. Unless his senses are dulled by perverse education, he will detect that peculiar musty smell which always indicates more danger to the sick than there is safety contained in the long list of benevolent and eminent physicians and expert surgeons who attend in the wards. Let him go into the surgical wards and ask whether wounds heal kindly, whether operations succeed, whether hospital gangrene ever appears, whether erysipelas is common, whether purulent ulcerations and discharges are apt to take place?

In the new surgical part of the Edinburgh Infirmary he will be answered that "Hospital gangrene is never out of the wards." In the double wards of Guy's Hospital, in London, he will be told that they are only fit for medical cases. In the Scutari hospitals, he would have learned that out of 44 secondary amputations, 36, or upwards of 80 per cent. died; that in one month there have been recorded 80 cases of hospital gangrene!

To place patients in musty wards is simply to kill them, with the addition of torture. We are confirmed in all these views by the published opinions of one to whom the world is indebted, and of whom human nature may be proud—Miss Nightingale.

CHAPTER XIV.

GREAT are the sacrifices made at the altar of Ignorance: 100,000 persons in England, says the Registrar-General, in his return for the Christmas quarter of 1858, died in the year before their time —died unnaturally. And yet (mark this) twice as many soldiers at home die every year as would be the case if the rate of mortality amongst them were *only* as great as amongst the general population. The general population die long before their time, but our soldiers, trained at great cost, are killed off, when they are at home at ease, more than twice as fast as the members of unwholesome trades; such, for example, as night printers. Compared with the members of friendly societies in agricultural districts, says the recent report of the commissioners appointed to inquire into the regulations affecting the sanitary condition of the army, the mortality of the Guards is three times and one-third greater; in other words, while there are six deaths and a little more per annum in 1,000 members of friendly societies, there are twenty deaths and a little more in 1,000 of the Guards! The principal agent is disease of the respiratory organs, and the leading cause of this disease is overcrowding in ill-ventilated and, often, ill-arranged and ill-drained barracks. Here we come back to the old story,—the story we have told so oft,— the story which the world listens to, and, shrugging its shoulders, still disbelieves. Men must have pure air. Feed them, clothe them,

protect them from the weather,—still, without a proper quantity of
fresh air, all is of no avail, and they rot and rot, and drop and drop.

When an English gentleman has reared and trained a pack of dogs,
or a lot of race-horses, he takes care they shall have a kennel or
a stable, as the case may be, wherein they will get this pure air, and
have all other circumstances in favour of their complete development.
When the English nation, at much larger expense, has produced a
body of trained soldiers,—soldiers, with souls, by the way, which the
dogs and the horses have not,—it might be supposed the governors of
the nation would, at any rate, take the same pains. So far from this
being the case, the men are placed under conditions infinitely worse
than if they had been left in their native hovels or garrets, and are
absolutely killed off, as was said just now, twice as quickly as they
ought to be, and that without the interposition of any foreign enemy.
The rooms are very confined, the beds are packed in close together,
the windows are insufficient and ill-placed ; where there are ventila-
tors, they are so actively .offensive, that the men risk the unfelt
danger and stop them; and thus the soldier sleeps in poison, and dies
in consequence.

Even in the most recently erected barracks in the metropolis the
arrangements are anything but efficient. We have found the air, in
the staircases, passages, and some of the rooms in the new buildings put
up for soldiers within the walls of the Tower of London, more stagnant and offensive than in any London prison that we ever went
into.

The report lately issued reiterates all that the writer had said
elsewhere on the arrangements of hospitals, recommending the plan
of separate pavilions, with windows on opposite sides, and natural ventilation ; and confirmed the objections made to the proposed arrangement of the great hospital at Netley. Leaving the report, however,
we prefer to look for ourselves at one or two of the London barracks,
and, following our own plan, to appeal to the eye as well as the
understanding of our readers, by means of the pencil.

The *Portman-street Barracks* will serve the purpose. But for the
small boys and patient maidens loitering round the entrance on the
east side of the street, it might be supposed to lead to stables or
a builder's yard ; yet here accommodation (?) is provided for about
500 of our best troops. Built more than a century ago for cavalry
soldiers, it is said, it is now occupied by foot guards, many of the
men being in the apartments originally intended for the horses. On
the north and south sides of a paved parallelogram are the soldiers'
dwellings; on the west are the officers' rooms ; and, on the east,
a large building, which was formerly a riding-school, but is now used
as a cooking and dining room. With the exception of the place last
mentioned, the buildings are two stories in height, and the most striking
feature is the small amount of window-opening. In the square are
several pumps, which formerly supplied the soldiers with water from
wells. These are now little used, and large cisterns, sufficient for the

purpose, have been erected, which are filled by the ordinary water service.

On entering one of the dwelling-rooms of the men, which are nearly all alike, we find on the ground-floor a scene that resembles the accompanying drawing. The sketch was made when the soldiers were

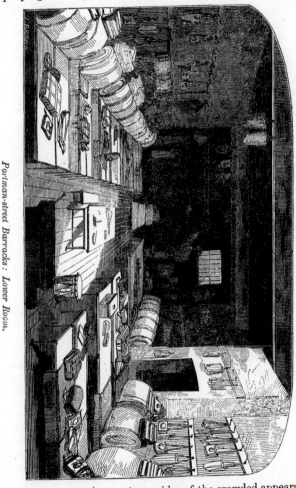

Portman-street Barracks: Lower Room.

away at dinner, and does not give an idea of the crowded appearance of the place when from twenty to twenty-two men are assembled in it. In the ceiling of the apartment are four small openings to square wooden shafts, passing from the ceiling through the room above to a cowl on the roof. The small window at the further end of the apartment is, like many of the others, within a few feet of neighbouring houses, and affords but a gloomy light, which is not much eclipsed by that from the window in the front. With both these aids the place is far too dark for either health or cleanliness. The iron bedsteads are arranged two and two, close together, and between each two there is a space of not more than a couple of feet. As regards the ventilating holes in the ceiling, they are not covered by perforated zinc, nor have any means been used to distribute the air gradually through the apartments. It is not surprising, therefore, that the soldiers who sleep near these holes say that they are seldom without a bad cold. One man here was so hoarse that he could scarcely speak, and others were not much better. The result doubtless is, that, to avoid this evil, an old jacket is made to provide a remedy, and, at the same time, to deprive the occupants of the rooms of all means of ventilation except the chimney-opening, and this, in some instances, has been contracted until it is not larger than that of a small room in an ordinary dwelling, because of the smoke. More than one soldier spoke of these barracks in summer as the " Black-hole of Calcutta," and no wonder.

We did not need to be told that, when the room is occupied at night, it requires strong nerves on the part of one who would put his nose into it. It seems extraordinary, remembering that there are medical officers attached, that such a state of things should be permitted to exist. Is it that they have a difficulty in making themselves heard by those whose business it is to remedy such evils, or does custom blunt observance? The number of occupants should, of course, be lessened, so long as the place is occupied at all for such a purpose, and then some improvements might be made by simple means. For example, instead of allowing the current from the shafts to descend on the sleeping soldier, a circular plate of metal suspended beneath the opening near to the ceiling would distribute it, and render it less dangerous. To make the shafts serve the purpose of *removing the vitiated atmosphere,* for which they were probably introduced, fresh air must be brought in elsewhere.

In the upper room the roof is in two spans, the ventilation-shafts already mentioned passing through it. The supports at the intersection of the roofs are only 8 feet high. An intelligent non-commissioned officer, who had carefully calculated the amount of space, said that there were not more than 180 cubic feet of space for each man, and with this limited amount (about a fourth of what it should be) no effective ventilation.* Here is the same arrangement of windows, which fails sufficiently to illuminate the apartment. There was no fire in this room, the men saying that the allowance of coals for each room was so small that they were obliged to husband them.

The closets are in a very unwholesome state, and must endanger the sentinels who all the night stand by some of them;—even if the mischief stop there.

---

* The appendix to the report gives 331 cubic feet as the space to each man in these barracks. Admit this, and it is not half enough for life.

Before leaving the place, it should be mentioned that some of the living-places provided for the married non-commissioned officers consist of a single room. The sergeant-major, for example, has a wife and four children, the eldest a great girl of fourteen, and all are forced to sleep in the same room, and that room, too, the one they live in. A drain passes underneath this apartment, and in summer renders it unbearable. Health cannot possibly be maintained under such circumstances. Truly, as Hood sings,—

> " Evil is wrought by want of head,
>   As well as want of heart."

Married non-commissioned officers should be provided with a living and sleeping room : moreover, the damp condition of some of these dwellings, which is disgraceful, should be remedied. It is said, however, when these matters are remarked upon, that "the barracks have been condemned for the last five-and-thirty years, so that it is useless to talk about improving them." And all this time our soldiers have been kept in a place and under conditions where healthful life is impossible. The existence of hundreds has been shortened, and the health of all damaged. Mere overcrowding, under otherwise good circumstances, produces enervation, disease, and death. An illustration is afforded by M. Boudin, in the "*Annales d'Hygiène Publique*," quoted by Dr. Balfour, which it may be worth while to state briefly, although it is discreditable to the age that any fresh instances should be needed. M. Boudin found that every year, from 1843 to 1847, about the month of October, there was a murderous epidemic of typhoid fever in the military hospital at Versailles, exclusively among the sick soldiers who came from the garrison of St. Cloud. It was the more remarkable, inasmuch as it always showed itself about a week after the arrival of the then king at St. Cloud. What could be the cause of it ? It never attacked the civil population, the officers, nor even the lower officers, though the latter occupied the same barracks as the soldiers who were attacked. The cause was simply overcrowding. Ordinarily the garrison consisted of 400 or 500 men, and had scarcely any sick. When the king came, the number was increased to 1,200 ; the men were closely packed in small ill-ventilated chambers, and were soon prostrated by fever, from which the non-commissioned officers, better fed, less fatigued, and never sleeping more than two in one room, altogether escaped !

"But," it may be said, "all this, as to Portman-street, was said in the *Builder* exactly one year ago. Surely, by this time, the evils pointed out have been remedied ?" Not in the slightest degree. We went into the barracks a few days ago (February), and found it in precisely the same state as before !

Long before the Commissioners who have recently reported were appointed, the writer had said that "if full examination of all barracks in which British troops are quartered were ordered, and a truthful report drawn up, the world would be startled at the horrible revelations made;" and asserted that "there are barracks in which the soldiers are never healthy, and hospitals in which the sick never get well." This will be believed now, though it was scoffed at then. The evils of the ill-constructed and overcrowded barrack-room cannot be mitigated by its tenants, and are constant in their operation, lowering health, and ultimately destroying life.

There is no reason why barracks should be less healthy than ordinary habitations, but the reverse. In the model lodging-houses of the metropolis, arranged with a view to health, the rate of mortality is not half so large as it is amongst the general population. "To the objection," says the *Times*, in one of the series of able articles in which it sought to bring forcibly before the general public the report of the Commissioners—"to the objection that these results are only shown in buildings which, like the model lodging-houses, have been constructed expressly with a view to health, the Commissioners justly reply that a regard for health should govern the construction of barracks also. Their present inferiority to the common lodging-houses, the casual refuge of the tramp, the outcast, and the vagabond, does not admit even this poor apology; the object of the owners or 'farmers' of this class of houses was only to obtain the largest possible amount of nightly rent from the largest number of inmates. Yet 'due intelligence,' invested with due power, has purified their abominations, spite of all defects of construction. The military authorities have required no addition of powers, no Acts of Parliament, no delegation of functions to the police; they have no opposition from greedy landlords to overcome; yet the state of things under their control is what the report describes. In truth, the whole of this section of the document is a strong indictment of the War Department, as proprietors and keepers of soldiers' lodging-houses, for permitting all the nuisances proscribed by the Act regulating the lodging-houses of the metropolis."

Continuing our examination, let us look at *St. George's Barracks*, one entrance to which is afforded by the westernmost opening through the National Gallery, in Trafalgar-square. There is a considerable open space here, and the barracks have the reputation of being amongst the best in the metropolis. The accommodation provided for the men consists in a long range of buildings, four stories high, above the ground, with rooms below the surface, not used at present for dwellings, but for pipe-claying and other cleansing operations. The whole length of the building is divided into separate parts, which have distinct entrances, both from the front and back. The staircases are wide, and on the right and left are apartments, each of which forms a home for sixteen or seventeen men. These rooms are fitted with the necessary number of beds. The soldiers' arms and other accoutrements are hung around. A large table is in the centre; and so closely are the beds placed together, that when they are prepared for the night, but little room is left for moving about. The published return gives 390 cubic feet as the space allowed for each man,—not half what it should be. The fact is, however, that the provision of cubic space alone is not sufficient : there must be *area*, the beds must be at a greater distance apart. The rooms are not more than 11 feet in height ; the windows are at each end of the rooms, and admit sufficient light, but all of them were closed. There is also a fireplace in each apartment ; and, with the exception of this, the only other means of ventilation are four apertures (closed) in the ceiling of each room, which communicate with a grating in the outer wall ; and, as there is no other arrangement for bringing *in* air, of course operate in that way instead of in removing the vitiated air. And, the rooms being comparatively low, this method of letting in air is objected to by most of the soldiers, who say that when lying in bed those near the openings are constantly catching cold, in consequence of the wind blowing down upon them in a current.

At about eleven o'clock in the morning, although a considerable number of the soldiers were out at drill, the atmosphere of the rooms, which serve for the purpose of both sleeping and dining, was heavy and offensive ; doors and windows were closed, and the stagnated condition of the air proved that the ventilation by the ceiling was quite insufficient. In the wards of St. Bartholomew's Hospital, even in the winter time and at night, some of the windows are kept open at the top, the authorities knowing that there is more danger, even as

St. George's Barracks : the Reading-room.

regards diseases of the lungs, from polluted air, than from a plentiful supply of wholesome air.

There is a library in the barracks, and we were glad to learn that when they are fully occupied as many as 300 soldiers subscribe towards its support. The pleasure of a visitor, however, is damped, on visiting the library, to find it placed in an apartment of the same size as the sleeping-rooms already mentioned, and just as much care taken there to exclude the air as in the other places. The Reading-room,—or rather, as we should say, the reading *without* room,—is represented by our sketch. The place was crowded, some were reading, others playing at dominoes and similar games. A thick crowd stood round the fire, and the scene was at any rate very picturesque. We are told that in wet or bad weather (when the air is more oppressive than usual), from 150 to 200 soldiers will take shelter here and amuse themselves. It seems extraordinary that in this enlightened age the medical officers of a regiment should allow such a number to congregate in so inadequate a space, so ill cared for as regards ventilation. In the prisons no such defiance of those sanitary arrangements which are necessary for the preservation of health is permitted.

The library and reading-room should be at least twice its present size, and properly ventilated, and then it might be a place where the men could pleasantly and usefully spend their spare hours. As it is at present, they get more harm than good by attending there.

There is here a school for teaching both the adults and children of the regiment, and an infant school : in the latter, both space and ventilation are insufficient.

The closets are ranged at the back of the barracks, at no great distance from the windows, and are flushed *once a day*, by means of a contrivance which throws in a large quantity of water ; but during a whole day and a night matters are allowed to remain in a condition manifestly dangerous, when we consider that at times from 700 to 1,000 persons are lodged here.

While examining these arrangements, and making inquiries of the men, we could not avoid comparing the improved intelligence of the soldiers of the present day with that of the veterans of the long war : nevertheless, the efforts of our army in the Crimea and elsewhere show that increased knowledge and better habits have not lessened their bravery and power of endurance.

The *Tower of London*, rich in associations, and which from a remote time has been amongst the most noted of the strongholds of England, has, during the last twenty or thirty years, undergone great changes. Long ranges of buildings have been placed on the site of those destroyed by the last fire, and these, like many other modern fortresses, remind one most of the scene-painter's conventional Gothic castle. In one point of view, nevertheless, improvement has been made in the arrangements of these barracks, which are much better than some which have been mentioned. The rooms are larger, and the number of men in each less, and here we find the natural results. The ratio of deaths is, nevertheless, much too high.

In addition to the overcrowded living-rooms, great damage is done in the guard-rooms, which are too small for the purpose of holding at times from forty to fifty men during the night. In some of these places doors and windows are closed, and there is no other ventilator than the chimney. Wooden boxes, like those in the casual wards of workhouses, are provided for the men to rest upon, and in wet weather they often lie down in their wet cloaks, and the place becomes filled with steam and other unwholesome vapours. Our sketch shows the guard-room at Portman-street at night, as sketched on the spot.

The Guard-room at Night, Portman-street Barracks.

The accommodation for married soldiers requires great alteration. In the lodging-houses of the metropolitan poor, the strong arm of the law has been called on to stop the demoralizing practice of over-

Married Soldiers' Quarters, Albany-street Barracks.

crowding, and persons who allow several families to live promiscuously in the same apartment are now liable to fine and imprisonment. In the houses of the soldiers such arrangements are still permitted as set all the rules of decency at defiance. One room is insufficient for a married couple and five or six children, and where only one room is provided, a partition should, at any rate, be so placed as not to interfere with the space ; but in Portman-street and other places, this does not seem to have been thought of ; and, bad as is this arrangement for the non-commissioned officers, there is worse as regards the privates, who are lodged two or more families in one small room, with *no other separation than curtains* drawn round the bed. Anything more demoralizing or destructive to the self-respect of men, women, and children, could not well be imagined,—nothing can stand against its effects. We have sketched a room occupied by three married soldiers, over the stables in the Albany-street Barracks.

It seems extraordinary that such things should be allowed ; but, so far as we can learn, little trouble has been taken by the superior officers generally to examine the dwellings of the men. In London, most of the chief officers live away from the barracks, and it is to be feared that some of the medical men have not been sufficiently thoughtful ; others, as we know, have long striven to obtain improvement, but without success.

The abomination of compelling soldiers to take their food and spend their spare time in the apartments in which a crowd of them have passed the night, should no longer be permitted. A greater amount of space should be given to each man, drainage should be made perfect, and the means of efficient ventilation afforded. Covered ambulatories are much wanted : some of the ancient barracks, as at Pompeii, had the parade-ground surrounded by a covered gallery, and here, too, there was a theatre for the amusement of the men in leisure time.

One-half of the hard drinking, says the late Sir Charles Napier,

"springs from the discomfort, the despair caused by bad barracks ;" and again, —"Losses by battle sink to nothing, compared with those inflicted by improperly constructed barracks and the *jamming* of soldiers, — no other word is sufficiently expressive."

Enervated by bad air, without sufficient occupation, and destitute of elevating

Black Hole for the Cavalry, Knightsbridge Barracks.

motive, the soldier is morally *swamped*, and dies in the slough,— a worse "black hole" than even that appropriated to the cavalry in Knightsbridge barracks, which has no means of ventilation but the small grate shown in the engraving. If a man is to be punished, there is no reason why you should sap his health and lessen his efficiency for good.

Some people say that it would not be wise to destroy the hardihood of the men, by making them too comfortable in barracks, as that would cause them to bear badly the difficulties of a campaign. This is surely erroneous. Agricultural labourers are best able to carry out their work, and endure the changes of the weather, if they are properly fed and lodged in well-drained and well-ventilated houses. So the soldier will be fittest to battle with both the enemy and the pestilence, who has not had his constitution undermined by months of residence in overcrowded and unwholesome rooms, which serve the purposes of eating, and sleeping, and killing. The wholesale murder which has been going on must no longer be permitted.

It is very difficult to induce the adoption of a new step. Immediately on the occurrence of the mutiny in India in 1857, the writer urged the immediate organization of a sanitary commission to proceed to India with our army, but nothing has been done in that direction.

A Parliamentary report as to the deaths in the Baltic and Black Sea fleets, shows that the deaths in both fleets, in the years 1854 and 1855, numbered 2,029, of which 1,574 were the result of disease, 228 of suicide, drowning, and other accidental causes, and only 227 of wounds in action. These figures show that in our navy, as in the army, pestilence and disease are far more fatal than the sword or artillery, and the other perils of war. The deaths by various diseases amounted to upwards of 7 to 1 of those which were caused by battle.

The report states that if the Baltic fleet had not anchored in Baro Sound during the summer of 1854, and if the fleet in the Black Sea had shunned Baljick and Varna in July, August, and September of the same year, the ravages by cholera would have been very much lessened. We also learn that there is no evidence to show that the climate and soil of the steppes of the Crimea had the least effect in producing complaints approximating to cholera ; but that accumulated filth and effluvia, arising from the decay of organic matter, brought their sure and deadly results.

In the Crimean armies, the number of those who died from disease was immense in comparison with those who fell in the various conflicts. This is the case in all campaigns. A competent authority stated that a quarter of the British army engaged in the Indian war would fall by fever, cholera, dysentery, and similar complaints. Many of the chiefs of that army have already perished by these agencies, and thousands of men. In the Crimea these were more deadly foes than the Russians.

If, then, we find that the pestilence is more terrible than the enemy, it is evidently necessary that we should have commanders and officers as capable of fighting the one as the other. During the long continental war, forty or fifty years ago, the principles of sanitary science

were but little understood; and even at the present time, we fear
that the sure means of saving life by a proper attention to those laws
which prevent many fatal complaints are still too little understood,
or even believed in, by the leaders of our fleets and armies. Terrible
as are all the horrors of war, there is no phase of it more dreadful to
contemplate than the probable death of 250 out of each 1,000 strong
men who form our army in India,—not while aiding the actual object
in view,—not in the excitement of battle and with the glory of success,—but helplessly and unnecessarily, in camps and hospitals,
stricken down by rotting matter,—killed by want of sufficient pure
air!—and these not the aged, the delicate, or those of tender years,
who contribute such a large per-centage of the ordinary deaths in our
population, but men in the prime of manhood.

At the present time in the metropolis and large cities the death of
40 persons in the 1,000 per annum is considered, and rightly, a very
great excess: it is little short of murder, indeed! In some of the
model buildings of London, inhabited by families, the number of
deaths in the year is 16 in the 1,000. Out of the sixteen above
mentioned, if the average number of infants' deaths be the same
as among those belonging to a similar class in the metropolis, we
should have nearly half of the deaths under five years. This shows
the value of mature lives, and that every care must be taken to save
them; especially, says the financier, when we recollect what it costs
the country to send each man to India.

Sanitary management must be greatly improved, and ere long
become one of the chief arts of warfare. The time is not far distant
when an admiral will rather place his ships within the range of over-
powerful batteries than in positions which ensure the presence of
pestilence; and that in the choice of places for encampments, the
sanitary condition of sites will be held in nearly as much consideration as their military fitness.

At a time of great distress, a body of sanitary officers were sent
from England to endeavour to stay the plagues which beset the camp
before Sebastopol, and much advantage resulted from the step. This
of itself, with the clear evidence which we have at home of the fact,
that by knowledge and exertion thousands of valuable lives may
be saved, should lead at once to what we are calling for, namely, the
*appointment of a distinct and sufficiently powerful body of sanitary
officers, and also of workmen to carry out their instructions, to attend
the army in India.* We believe that such a corps properly organized,
would, in a region like India, be the means of adding immensely to
our available force. It is true that many of our army surgeons are
quite capable of giving advice on this subject, but we have reason to
know that their opinions do not meet with sufficient consideration;
and, moreover, the calls upon their attention during a campaign leave
them little time for additional duties.

Thousands will die in India unnecessarily, if the course here
pointed out be not pursued.

CHAPTER XV.

OUR allies on the other side of the Channel, or at all events some of them, are arriving at the conclusion that their system of house-building, piling flat upon flat, and accumulating under the same roof large numbers of persons of widely different positions in society, is inferior to the mode pursued in England, where each house is built to accommodate a single family,—though, in the majority of cases, we must add, for the information of French friends, it is afterwards *made to contain several.* In a volume published in Paris by M. Felix Abate, architect, " *Sur la Nécessité d'une double Réforme de l'Archi-tecture Domestique en France, spécialement appliqués à la Classe moyenne et ouvrière,*" the author,—who desires, first, to change the arrangement of houses, and, secondly, to lessen the cost of lodging,— enumerates the various inconveniences attendant on the French system,—the loss through making one apartment the passage-way to another, the lack of conveniences, the want of light and ventilation, the absence of tranquillity and privacy. With these he contrasts our small houses, built each for a single family, or so arranged (as he maintains, oddly enough) that each room on a floor communicates with the staircase, so that the house may be divided into various little lodgings. Certainly, if a house is to be occupied by more than one family, the French and Scotch mode of construction is infinitely preferable to the English ; giving, as it does, to each tenant his own door of entrance, and to each flat the various conveniences required by a family. Nevertheless, we are far from advocating the superiority of the French house-upon-house system : we simply desire that in smaller houses, the appropriation of which may be foreseen, proper arrangements should be made to secure the privacy,—the domestic sanctity—so much prized by English people, and so valuable in the maintenance of the national character.

This problem of cheap, healthful dwellings is, indeed, one of the immensest importance. The first step towards it is to make known what a healthful dwelling is. Bermondsey,—Bermundesye, or Beor-mund's eye, as it was anciently called, showing its watery neighbour-hood,—is flat and unfavourable for draining operations : and whenever cholera has visited the metropolis, it has made fearful ravages in Bermondsey. Until lately it has been much neglected.

After passing Tooley-street, from London-bridge, the visitor will find himself amongst wide and airy-looking streets of small houses, many of them built during the last twenty or thirty years. Here and there a few close courts of ancient wooden houses contrast strongly with the less picturesque dwellings.

Jacob's Island has been improved, but many parts of the neighbour-hood are still in a miserable condition.

Following the road from Dock-head, guided by the finger-post directing towards the south entrance of the Thames Tunnel, you reach Blue Anchor-lane. Here there is a cottage—we will not name

The Brink of Evil.

A Choice Site for Houses.

it—where the cholera carried off several victims, nor need we wonder. It is ill-built, situated in a garden, and without drainage. Close to the house there was a pond, from which the gardeners took water; the cesspool overflowed into the pond, and soon after the cholera attacked the inhabitants, and three persons died. An open ditch passes along

Blue Anchor-lane, into which runs the water from the premises of some manufacturing chemists. We have been to Cologne, and have

"*Just dropped in.*"

a tolerably intimate acquaintance with Coleridge's seventy stenches; we are bound, nevertheless, to say, that this ditch has an odour peculiarly its own. Closely bordering on the ditch, as shown in the engraving, are eight or nine little cottages. Fever, of course, is well known here. Such a state of things requires no comment; and yet, strange to say, along the edge of this pestilent ditch new houses have been built, as shown in the second sketch. A few days ago, when we

passed the ditch, it was in a worse state than it was when we first
pointed out the error in placing houses in this position four years ago.

Looking at an entirely different but equally notorious suburb,—the
Potteries at Kensington,—we find little or no improvement has been
made there either. On the other side is a sketch of the actual appearance presented by a room in the neighbourhood during a shower of rain.
The pool known as " The Ocean" has been lessened, it is true, but the
pigs still flourish, all the efforts on the part of the medical officer to
obtain their removal having failed. Many cases have been prosecuted,
but up to this time the Nuisance Removal Act has been found insufficient : the condition of the people remains the same,—and life
continues to be wasted and dwarfed :—

"There is nothing 'strange' in your shortening breath : nothing
'mysterious' in your diminished days. Can a man take fire to his
breast and not be burned ? You have eaten sour grapes, and your
teeth are necessarily set on edge. Your path inclineth unto death,
and your roadways unto the dead."

CHAPTER XVI.

IF we harp too long on one string we may fail to hold our listeners.
Let us change it, and summon to view a Christmas party gathered
about the social hearth.

Hail, Christmas ! Bringer of pleasant thoughts, and awakener of
good feelings,—feelings so buried in some under the dry leaves of the
world, that were they not stirred by thee, their existence would be
unknown ! Apart from thy greatest claim to the attention of man,
—the hopes and promises belonging to thee,—how much delight does
the world owe thee,—how many coldnesses has thy genial flame—the
flame of charity—dispelled ! As a new poet sings :—

> " Mere contact makes not nearness : they who sit
>   On the same hearth are often more apart
>   Than those who have a bulging hemisphere
>   Rising between them."—J. E. JACKSON.

And by the force of memory, the force of example, and the force of
association, Christmas brings the separated together, and teaches others
that there is happiness within the reach of all, and that "it needs not
fortune to be great :"—

> " We know not half we may possess,
>   Nor what awaits, nor what attends :
> We're richer far than we may guess,—
>   Rich as eternity extends !
>
> The heart it hath its own estate,
>   The mind it hath its wealth untold ;
> It needs not fortune to be great,
>   While there's a coin surpassing gold !"—C. SWAIN.

The very Wassail bowl says,—" Be in health* (though we are not recommending an indulgence in it), and the Mistletoe was called by the Druids " All-heal." Look, on Christmas Eve, into one of the old homesteads scattered about the country : see the pleasant party to which we have referred,—old and young, grave and gay, worldly and spiritual,—gathered about the wide open fire-place, still to be found, with its blazing logs on the old fire-dogs : care banished, jealousy and ill-feelings forgotten, and those to whom aid or sympathy may be useful remembered. Multiply this by millions, and some idea will be gained of the value of Christmas. The talk of the group here sketched, not an imaginary one, was varied. Some spoke

> ————" About the plan
> And method of the universe ; and plunged
> In difficulties on the politics
> And civil laws of Saturn ; weaving webs
> Of lofty speculation in their minds
> To bridge across the gulf-like infinite,
> And suffer them to crawl o'er,—spider-wise."

But some were frightening each other about the " death-watch " and " winding-sheets," and other asserted foretokens of death ; and it led us to think on what foundations these superstitious notions might have been built—notions which even now are, to a certain extent, enter-tained by many persons. For, though the bulk of the population may exclaim with Crabbe,—

> " But lost, for ever lost, to me, those joys
> Which reason scatters, and which time destroys !
> No more the midnight fairy tribe I view,
> All in the merry moonshine tippling dew ;
> E'en the last lingering fiction of the brain,—
> The churchyard ghost,—is now at rest again :"—

still hundreds believe that the ticking of the " death-watch," or the appearance of a crow near a dwelling, foretells an approaching disso-lution. May it not be that there is a groundwork of truth for the association ? Sanitary knowledge supplies some reasons for thinking so. The little beetle has often by its clicking caused terror to many who have defied, unchanged, obvious and great dangers. This creature chiefly carries on its operations in the night-time, and is, in conse-quence, the more likely to be heard by the watchers of the sick ; but, besides this, it is seldom found in thoroughly ventilated rooms, though frequently in damp, mildewed apartments, or in decayed wood-work, —places, in fact, which are generally so conditioned as to be unfavour-able to health and life ; and it is not impossible that in early days, when knowledge of sanitary laws was small, there were sufficient reasons to connect the " death-watch " with numerous instances of death.

The howling of a dog at night near the home of the sick is con-

* Wæes hæl.—" Health-liquor,"—" Be in health."

sidered, like the ticking of the "death-watch," an ominous sign, and this, too, may be accounted for on sanitary grounds; for, in many cases which end in death, the sick room, even if great care be taken, is pervaded with an impure atmosphere which tells of dissolution. Of course those gases are distributed abroad, and no animal is more keen-scented than the dog. The wolf will rush to its food for miles with a precision that seems marvellous, but which is owing to the fineness of its smell; and the dog is but a civilized wolf, obeys the instinct of its species, and is led by the taint of the air.

The "winding-sheet" in the candle is another token which creates fear in superstitious minds. The melting and hardening of the tallow, in the form which has this name, is caused by draughts of air, which are dangerous to all, especially the delicate. In those old times, when there was more reason than at present to connect death with the "winding-sheet" in the candle, the practice of swaddling infants in an absurd amount of clothing, the close curtains of bedsteads, and other similar causes, often rendered the draught of air which produced the "winding-sheet" of the candle as deadly in its effect as powerful poison or revengeful blow.

> " Who gets the wind but through a hole,
> May make his will and mind his soul."

Ventilation does not consist of such currents of air as will produce this effect on the candle.

We have alluded to another superstition, which is still common in many parts of England, namely, that it is a sign of ill-health, at the least, for a carrion-crow or a raven to alight near a dwelling. It is well known that these birds can detect impurity of the atmosphere from a great distance. Vultures and carrion-crows will assemble in hundreds, from different quarters, by the body of a dead horse or other animal; and it is, therefore, not going far out of the way to connect their visits to a human residence with some impure taint of decaying matter which is there collected.

The ghostly phantoms of marshy districts, the phosphoric lights which appear in various forms rising from the surface of pools in which decomposing bodies are lodged, churchyard lights, and horrible dreams, are all attendants of evil sanitary conditions, and may well have come to be regarded as foretelling sickness or death.

The cracking of furniture, too, which is by some regarded as a warning of death, is no doubt often heard before such an event. Watchers listen with nervous ears to all sounds; and, as the cracking of the woodwork in churches and houses is caused by a sudden change in the atmosphere, which may operate badly on the sick, death often rapidly follows such sounds, and so this superstition has grown up.

When it has seemed to *rain blood*, it has been viewed as a portent of evil and death : and with truth. Observation has proved that the spots were those of a red fungus, the concomitant, says Dr. Daubeny, of epidemics and the failure of crops. These evils had occurred where the spots had been, and were, therefore, expected when the red spots again made their appearance.

We might pursue the subject much further, but must stop here, seeking but to awaken attention, through a fresh means, to the importance of attention to sanitary laws and requirements, and to transform hobgoblins and portents into kindly warnings not lightly to be disregarded.

CHAPTER XVII.

MUCH credit is due to Mr. Slaney, with others, for continuous endeavours to improve the condition of the masses. Amongst his good works must be placed his Bill (without admitting all its details) to facilitate the grant of land near populous places for the regulated recreation of adults and as playgrounds for poor children ;—notwithstanding that it was difficult to keep "a house" while he was moving for leave to bring it in. He pointed out that the changes which had taken place in various directions for the benefit of all other classes of society had operated to the injury of the labouring poor, by driving them to reside within a narrower area, and by not having reserved places for exercise and recreation. He had drawn the attention of the House of Commons to this, he said, twenty-five years ago, and had obtained a committee upon the question, and the report which that committee had made contained suggestions, many of which had been since adopted. We sincerely hope that the object will not be lost sight of. Wholesome recreation for adults is amongst the necessaries of life : and as to the poor *children* of London and other large towns, it is scarcely possible to over-estimate the degradation and money loss brought about by confining them to the wretched homes of their parents or the more wretched haunts of the thousands of town children who have no parents or protectors to overlook them. You may often see children, dwellers in the close courts and alleys which in many cases adjoin our nicely planted squares, the home of fashion, following the instincts of nature, creeping from the shadow to the fresher air and sunshine, and eagerly peeping through the enclosures at the shrubs and flowers, till driven back by stalwart street-keepers and policemen, when they scamper off to their dingy homes, where, in too many instances, contamination awaits them. In confined streets the children are without the means of healthful amusement, or of any chance of occupying their time and leading their thoughts in such a manner as would be likely to strengthen the body or cultivate the faculties. They cannot, like little George Stephenson, ramble to the " burn," and amuse themselves in constructing miniature water-mills, or dig clay from the bog, and gather the stems of hemlocks and fashion the materials into engines. A rightly-formed heart must ache for the poor boys and girls of London, particularly when it is recollected what multitudes of them there are who are progressing towards manhood and womanhood deteriorated and educated downwards. To many of them the glorious tints of the setting sun are a sight scarcely known, and to them the "rosy hue of incense breathing morn" must be as strange as the fresh green places in which children in the country have an opportunity of cheerfully spending their play-hours. Who has heard without delight the joyous voices and the rush into lanes and fields of the children of the village schools—how different from the dismissal from the schools of the poor in parts of London—to many of whom a large dust-heap, the embankment made when opening a sewer, or some similar arena, is a treat of an extraordinary description. Priceless are the recollections of those green lanes and flowery banks in after days, as when,—

> " In vacant or in pensive mood,
> They flash upon that *inward eye*
> Which is the bliss of solitude."

Those who are acquainted with the subject know the evil which follows from allowing children to play in the streets. "What can we do ?" say the parents : "it is natural for children who are in health to play, and how can they do so in their inconvenient room, without quarrels with the neighbours ?" They must swarm into the streets, and risk the great dangers which await them. It is absolutely necessary that some means should be taken to remedy this evil, and afford the means of such healthy exercise as can be had in the midst of a large population. In order to show this, glance at the dense population which inhabits the district from St. Martin's-lane to Farringdon-street, and between Oxford-street and Holborn, and the Strand and Fleet-street, and notice how few breathing-places are left for the use of the many thousands who occupy that space. To those living in the western portion, St. James's-park and the area in front of the National Gallery are not at a great distance ; but only few of the poorest avail themselves of those very public places ; and many have remarked with wonder how small a number of children from pent-up places make use of the parks. This is to be partly accounted for by the circumstance that the ill-clad are often looked at with suspicion. Moreover, young children seldom stray far from home. The only other open spaces in this locality are Leicester-square, the centre of which is nearly covered by the Great Globe building ; Covent-garden Market,—a space generally occupied ; Clifford's-inn ; Lincoln's-inn-fields ; and Gray's-inn. In the latter there is a beautiful piece of ground, with large and venerable trees, which have an historical interest : and we venture to suggest that great benefit would be conferred by opening it to the public, as the authorities of the Temple have opened their garden, which is the only other uncovered space in this district worthy of notice. To the latter place, in the summer evenings, thousands of the wives and children of the working classes living around have resorted ; and it is worthy of notice that the most orderly conduct has been observed, and no damage has been done, although many children have been admitted, to either the grass or flowers. In the week-days, during both summer and winter, all persons decently dressed, with or without children, are admitted, and none have complained of noise or inconvenience. This ought to be an encouragement to the members of the other Inns to follow the example which has been set them by the Templars.

In connection with some of the metropolitan schools in some of the more open parts of London, space has been reserved as playgrounds for the scholars, some of which are fitted up with poles for gymnastic exercise. In the parish of St. Clement Danes, which is thickly built upon, substantial school-rooms have been erected in Milford-lane. There was, however, no ground to spare for a playground, but a sort of cage has been ingeniously thrown over the flat roof, which thus affords a safe and airy place for the children to play on.

The play-ground of Christ's School is, for the City, large and convenient; so is that of the Charter-house. Both these, however, want the gymnastic apparatus which has been so well fitted up in the grounds of University College. In the Regent's-park, near the south base of Primrose-hill, a gymnasium some time since was opened, and this we have seen in the summer time crowded with youths and boys. A person who seemed to have been an old soldier acted as superintendent : before dark the ropes and poles were taken down, and the company soon dispersed. Similar arrangements might be made in Hyde-park and the other parks. What seems, however, to be wanted, in addition to the matters already mentioned, are little plots of ground for public play-grounds, at convenient intervals, in the midst of our densest population ; and a society, whose offices are at No. 17, Bull-and-Mouth-Street, St. Martin's-le-Grand, has been formed to carry out this laudable object. The idea is worthy of all praise, although we are reluctantly forced to confess that in those localities in which such institutions are most needed, there will be difficulties to encounter, such as the great value of ground, and the objection which arises to the noise. As children grow up, other means of recreation should be made available. Any one who would devise a system of attractive, cheap, and innocent amusements for the poor, would further the cause of morality. All classes must have recreation. "Recreation," says Bishop Hall, "is intended to the mind, as whetting is to the scythe, to sharpen the edge of it, which otherwise would grow dull and blunt. He, therefore, that spends his whole time in recreation, is ever whetting, never mowing ; his grass may grow and his steed may starve : as, contrarily, he that always toils and never recreates, is ever mowing, never whetting : labouring much to little purpose."

It is related that when Tahiti first came under European influence, the missionaries, with pure but mistaken motives, interdicted all the native amusements. They made dancing, foot-racing, and athletic games punishable offences, and prohibited every species of national pastime, from the holding of floral festivals to the singing of traditional ballads. To the effects of this policy a recent traveller bears mournful testimony. He tells us that, "supplied with no amusements in the place of those forbidden, the Tahitians have sunk into a state of listlessness, and indulge in sensualities a hundred times more pernicious than all the games ever celebrated in the temple of Tanee."*

The ignorant condition of thousands of both sexes in London, notwithstanding what has been done by ragged schools lately, is a frightful fact to contemplate. They see the sky above their heads, but have no notion of its composition ; the rain falls, but they know not the cause ; the bread they eat, the coal that warms them, and the dingy brickwork of their courts and streets, convey no idea to them beyond what is presented to their untaught eyes. Their mind cannot wander to the waving corn-fields, or to the sources of the production of the familiar things by which they are surrounded. Of the simplest religious truths and moral principles, they know nothing. It may seem to some that we are making an over-coloured statement, but those connected with the police-courts of the metropolis, know well the numerous cases which are brought to their notice of children from ten to twelve years of age, or more, who are not capable of taking an oath, in consequence of want of understanding ; and those who have visited the poor districts of London can form a further idea of the extent of this evil.

It is evident that this absence of knowledge is in a great measure the result of the want of opportunity ; for although, in some instances, bad air and other evils have created a dull and morbid temperament even in the young, it cannot fail to be noticed by all who have studied the subject, that the desire in these poor neighbourhoods for knowledge of some kind is remarkable, and as the right kind does not present itself, it is not surprising to see with what activity they set about a description of education they would be much better without. The human mind in varied degrees must find something to occupy itself with, and if good cannot be had, it rushes to the bad.

It is a curious sight to notice groups of young boys, of from seven to nine years of age, engaged, with all the earnestness of mature years, in games of chance,—such as dice, pitch and toss, and even cards ; smoking short pipes, and betting in a manner that would seem to show an instinctive power of counting, although they know neither a letter of the alphabet nor the figures of arithmetic. But the eagerness and rapt attention here seen are as nothing compared with what is apparent at *a penny theatre*, the chief means of education to large bodies of boys and girls who will be men and women, and form part of the community. Much evil arises from these resorts ; nevertheless, we have a strong conviction that they are calculated to do more good than harm, and that it is not so desirable to interdict as to improve them, and render them a means of satisfying innocently that yearning for mental food to which we have alluded. The real nature of these

* Sawyer's Essay on "Popular Amusements."

places is little understood : but those who would suggest adequate remedies for the social evils which exist amongst a very large number of the long-neglected classes of the population, must thoroughly investigate and understand existing circumstances. A year ago, the performances at penny theatres consisted of singing, dancing, and a short piece, generally of a melodramatic kind ; or, in the season, a sort of pantomime. In some instances, the words of the songs were broad and improper. Since then, however, the police have overlooked them ; many have been closed ; all attempts at what may be called theatrical exhibitions have been stopped ; and the amusement offered now consists chiefly of the singing of popular street songs and negro melodies in characteristic costumes. Dancing of the most vigorous description is highly relished, as also are feats of strength and conjuring ; and it is remarkable how great an attraction chemical experiments have. The exhibition of laughing gas, or galvanism, has been, and still is, a standard portion of these exhibitions. The entertainments at some of these places which we have taken the pains lately to see, although not instructive, had not of itself any immoral tendency.

The point we have in view is to show the eagerness with which this sort of *education* is taken advantage of, and that it is in truth the only sort of instruction to which many can be made to attend. The apartment is full, and the appearance, seen from the stage, very striking. Here are infants in the arms of mothers who have scarcely passed the years of girlhood ; the "two years' child," with staring eyes and open mouth, is looking with wondrous intentness on the scene passing on the small, ill-decorated stage : mixed in the group are boys of elder growth, and a few very young girls ; there are, besides, youths from sixteen to twenty, dressed in as nearly as possible the same style, viz. : short coats of velveteen, or some other stout material, cord trowsers, caps, and showy neck-ties. The younger boys imitate as closely as may be the fashion of their elders, although some are but ragged copies. We saw few on any occasion who seemed over twenty years of age, excepting one or two broken-down old men, who strangely contrasted with those surrounding.

The drawing we have engraved, and which serves as our frontispiece, is not "fancy's sketch," but a true record. As we are not seeking to advertise these places, but to lead to their improvement, we need not give the locality of the structure. The first "house" was just over : we counted out 680 boys and girls, many of the worst possible character ; and there were nearly as many waiting, who went in immediately after. A third representation was to follow, and complete the night. The engraving shows the boxes (2d.), and part of the back row of the pit (1d.) We saw no impropriety then, or on any other occasion, and could find no greater difference between that place and Astley's than there is between Astley's and the Italian Opera-House. Of course, gazing at this youthful crowd, it is impossible to ignore the danger and mischief which lie beneath ; and it is saddening to reflect that this is only a small sample of some thousands scattered here and there over the metropolis, and who, in a great measure, have been reared in neglect. The peculiar education (if we may so call it) of this class requires unusual measures, and it may be observed that, although, under the circumstances, books are useless, yet paintings, music, and exhibitions which place a tale of interest before the eye, meet with ready appreciation, and in the absence of the power of deriving amusement from books, we are inclined to think that the penny theatres, as now managed, do more good than harm, and that they might be very greatly improved, not only with advantage to the owners of them, but also to the visitors. Some of our readers will recollect Dr. Livingstone's observation, that the views afforded by the magic-lantern were the only kind of knowledge he was asked twice for by the Africans.

It has been objected to these exhibitions that they bring large numbers of dangerous characters together, and expose the younger part to the bad instruction of the elder. The same objection was made to the Ragged Schools at their commencement, but does not seem to hold good.

In the neighbourhood of Whitechapel there are various exhibitions which are resorted to by crowds of the same description as visit the penny theatres : these are of an artistic nature : they consist of representations of places and incidents connected with the late war, and other stirring events, which are shown by panoramas and dissolving views. Views in the Holy Land and places connected with the sacred Scriptures are very popular. These humble art-exhibitions are highly spoken of by experienced City missionaries ; and we are told that such considerable sums of money are raised by the speculators that they are enabled to effect great improvements, and that the people are becoming more critical. These exhibitions for the poor ought to receive encouragement, the pictures and the short lecture being the only books many can understand.

It would be well if rooms could be provided for the purpose of having well-arranged and popular concerts at a small cost. Illustrated lectures on subjects of common interest would be well attended, and these would be a means in some measure of connecting the darkness which feels pleasure only in sensual amusements with the light of more advanced intellectual recreations.

When, however, such groups as those at present under consideration are seen, when we view them hovering around the outskirts of crowds, or assembled together in friendly groups in the Borough and elsewhere, or coming forth in thousands at executions or in times of tumult, the prospect of effecting much real good in this sturdy and dangerous army seems small ; but the greater is the necessity of preventing the young and the yet unborn from growing up in large numbers to recruit the force which is now arrayed against honest industry and order.

We must lift them out of the Swamps and encourage the erection of Social Bridges, however small, which lead in a right direction, and amongst these are public playgrounds for children and innocent recreations for adults. All should remember that,—" When God gives a blessing to be enjoyed, he gives it with a duty to be done ; and the duty of the happy is, to help the suffering to bear their woe."

CHAPTER XVIII.

FEW know what is actually around and about them. Not long ago Islington held a Social Science Congress, when several spirited addresses were made to a large audience, with the view of securing their co-operation "in the efforts now being made for the welfare of the working classes."

The vicar took for the subject of his observations, "the need of sympathy between the various classes of society," and urged, wisely, that a distinction should be drawn between those who honestly and independently lived by manual labour, and those who were in a condition of indigence and pauperism through extravagance and intemperance. These latter did not really belong to the working classes, and he believed that false sympathy with such persons was productive of great harm. Working men had heads as hard and hearts as sound as theirs, and many of them were twice as intelligent as some above them were. The vicar then mentioned several ways in which their sympathy with the industrious classes might find practical manifestation : baths, savings' banks, and early closing. He had found out one thing in connection with the working classes that had startled him a little, viz. that while irreligion was one of the causes that kept people away from church, it was by no means the most general cause. They didn't choose to come to be stared at in the middle aisle. He should like an Islington Exeter-hall, and believed one might easily be erected for £2,000 or £3,000 which would answer every purpose. The Rev. Joseph Haslegrave spoke on "the duty of providing places of recreation and instruction for the working classes ;" and in the course of his observations, told a story of a man who had attended a tea-meeting given at St. Peter's to the parents of the school-children. On the following Sunday he was at church, and on one of his acquaintances expressing surprise, he said, "Well, you see, he was so kind and familiar the other night at the tea-meeting, that I couldn't help giving him a turn to-day."

Then the secretary of the Mutual Provident Association showed very clearly the usefulness of that and similar institutions ; and the secretary of the Religious Tract Society discoursed "on the circulation of useful literature amongst the working classes," and urged the increase of the library of the Working Man's Institute. Many very proper sentiments were expressed, and as tending to form public opinion, this meeting, and all similar meetings, will be useful. No distinct object for immediate attainment, however, was held up ; no local instances of the evils resulting from wants pointed out by the speakers were quoted; and we are tempted, accordingly, to supply the deficiency, and give two illustrations, one in support of the speaker who urged the duty of providing means of wholesome recreation for the working classes and those beneath them; and the other, as an evidence of the want of knowledge on sanitary matters or thoughtlessness in respect of them, which exists amongst the very leaders and teachers themselves, and of the necessity for an extension of such knowledge.

It is a remarkable circumstance that, notwithstanding all that has been said on sanitary matters, vast numbers of houses are rising up every month in this metropolis built with a view to their occupation by single families, which, even from the time they are finished, are let in tenements to two or three. West of the Caledonian-road, in the parish of which we are speaking, are several streets recently built, one of nearly half a mile in length, in which not a dozen of the houses are let to single families. It may be, that the ground landlord, who has the power to partition out the land, may, in his anxiety for uniformity, make such requirements as prevent a builder from erecting any houses except on the old plan : if so, this may be worthy of consideration, but is not our present point.

A stranger visiting the neighbourhood would be surprised in the evening at the thickness of the population : in one street here, only newly built, we believe there is as much of poverty and overcrowding as in some of the worst of the old districts. When the next return of the Registrar-General is made, the population of this and other similar districts will surprise many. Well, behind some of these houses near the North-London Railway is a waste piece of land, once meadow, but now covered with various materials. In one part are rows of one-storied cottages, without plan, and of such a description as would not now be allowed to be built within the metropolitan district ; and here, while the bells of the neighbouring churches are ringing, may be heard the loud voices of various dealers, and may be viewed such groups as our engraving shows. When the sketch was made, the proprietors of swings and roundabouts were busy, and pitch and toss, shooting at targets for nuts, card playing, and other modes of gambling were being carried on. This Sunday congregation includes within it various classes, the worst of which contaminate the rest. Some will perhaps ask, why such gatherings are permitted by the police ;—but to this we need not reply. We are simply viewing it as an evidence, to some extent, that if the means of innocent recreation at proper times be not afforded to the struggling classes, and they are not led up to have some self-respect and fear of opinion, they will make unwholesome recreation for themselves.

Trace some of these to their miserable " homes," and then say if sympathy, guided by knowledge, be not needed to bridge a way for them out of the slough. Shamefully has society neglected its duty, and high is the price it has to pay for the neglect.

A SUNDAY-SCHOOL IN ISLINGTON: NINETEENTH CENTURY.

"*Teaching the young idea how to shoot.*"

The struggling classes in London are very various, and are only to be understood by personal investigation : endeavours to aid them, without knowledge of all the circumstances, will fail. The manner in which those who practise certain trades sink gradually lower and

lower, irretrievably, is very curious. And having no one to say
to them,—

> " Up, faint heart, confront thy sorrow !
> Know'st thou not whence thou mayst borrow
> Hope of brighter things to-morrow ?
>   Look the danger in the face.
>
> Hath gaunt poverty o'ertaken ?
> Have thy sunshine friends forsaken ?
> Let thy courage then awaken,
>   Look the danger in the face."

Having no one, we say, to strengthen or to cheer them, they yield to
circumstances, and are lost. We went not long ago, one Saturday
afternoon, into the house of a manufacturer of bird-cages, of different
sizes and patterns, and more or less ornamental. It was not far from
Clerkenwell-green, and nothing can be imagined worse of its kind than
the sanitary condition of the house. It was a scene of confusion too :
the family consisted of a man and his wife, two daughters of about
fifteen and eighteen years of age, several boys, from four to thirteen,
and an infant : all, with the exception of the child, were actively at
work. Some were straining and colouring the commoner description
of cages ; one was boring holes for the wires ; another threading and
fixing them ; the father was cutting and arranging the woodwork ;
others were polishing; the unfinished cages were strewed about the
beds, and the odour in the apartment was bad in the extreme. We
were told that, owing to competition, from the number of similar
manufacturers, after paying for materials, the united exertions of the
family, taking the average, did not realize more than from 20s. to 25s.
a-week, and that the prices were constantly declining, so that they
had to work more hours for the same sum.

In another place we found a man whose entire occupation was to
carve a plain scroll on the upper rail of chair-backs. The wood was
supplied by the wholesale chair-maker, and it was surprising with
what rapidity the man cut in the familiar device : the sand-papering
and polishing-up he left to his family. He complained that when the
times were bad, the warehouse-men got overstocked, and then the
work failed : but those who have capital, and can afford to wait, say
to the men, "I don't want rails, but if you like to make a certain
number at half-price, you may: it will be better than doing nothing ;"
and then it is the old story over again of the Spitalfields weavers and
the needle-women : "We are obliged to buckle to, by working harder,
to earn a crust ; but *the prices never get up again !*"

A maker of barometers remarked that some excellent workmen—
men not very thrifty, and at times therefore out of money—were
obliged to take their work, perhaps incomplete, to a person who dealt
in that way, and he, knowing their need, drove a good bargain, and
by that means reduced the price of the labour of others.

We might enter into particulars to show that japanners, and many other craftsmen who work at home, find their inability to hold their position against capital, and, although they use slighter work,* cannot make a sufficient income to enable them to support their families. Their foot is on the edge of the Slough. Who will build them a Bridge?

But we are being led away. Let us get back to our evidence that knowledge of sanitary laws is wanting where it might be looked for. And we show it in the shape of a view of an infant school not far from the site of the Sunday gathering. We do not willingly draw attention to it, for all the parties concerned in it are guided by the best intentions, and have to labour under very great difficulties. It is, however, absolutely necessary that such errors should be noticed, because they are full of danger, and, moreover, by directing attention to the eagerness with which education is caught at, it may cause re-

AN INFANT-SCHOOL IN FULL PLAY.

" The Breath of Man is fatal to his Fellows."

newed exertions to be made to enable the founders of infant and other schools in poor neighbourhoods to provide apartments of sufficient size to admit of breathing in. The health of infant children is of as great importance as the amount of instruction which can be given to them. In this school from seventy to eighty children assemble morning and afternoon, spending altogether five hours in two rooms

* A japanner, who exhibited some good specimens of his work, which contrasted curiously with the slight effects he was turning off at the time, reminded us of the story of the artist who was engaged to paint battle-scenes on tea-trays at so much a dozen. At first long rows of cavalry and infantry might be observed clearly delineated ; but, as the dealer lessened his price, the artist introduced more smoke and fewer figures, and so earned as much money ; and this went on, till the dealer, one day putting on his spectacles, found that there were no figures visible, and said,— " Why, sir, there is nothing left but smoke."

thrown together, each of which is 12 feet long by 12 feet wide, and 7 feet 6 inches high. In summer time a current of air can be passed through the room, but at the time of our visit—a rather chilly morning,—the windows were closed, and the air, as a matter of course, was polluted to such a degree that it was violently poisonous. Both pen and pencil will fail to give an idea of the overcrowded state of this school, and cheerfully and well, under the circumstances, as the teacher was doing her duty, it was evidently not easy to preserve order amongst so many children so closely packed. To make matters worse, the drainage of the neighbourhood is imperfect, and the houses have either open cesspools or such as are simply disguised.

There are many schools which are not better situated, and we would strongly advise those who may be engaged in planting new schools, beginning in a humble manner, to have careful advice as to the drainage. If possible, parts of small and ordinary dwelling-houses should be avoided. It is better to have some disused carpenters' shop, which, even with a coat of whitewash may be less sightly, but is infinitely more wholesome.

It would be difficult to estimate the amount of disease and misery engendered by such a state of things as is presented by the infant school we have illustrated, and we would have it clearly understood that our sketch is in no way "doctored," but is a faithful representation of the scene. Air once breathed is poison. Breathed more than once, it becomes surcharged with carbonic acid gas and other waste excretions of the body. "When the surcharge of impurity," says Dr. M'Cormac, "amounts to ten per cent. of carbonic acid gas, the respired air will take up no more waste. Here the waste is retained in the system, and if the evil process be continued, eventually leads to disease." One result of this, it is maintained, is *consumption*. It is quite true what Rousseau says,—"*L'haleine de l'homme est mortelle à ses semblables.*" Let us, then, call upon the estimable persons who interest themselves in the instruction of children to see that they have ample breathing space, and, amongst the things taught, let the rules necessary for healthful existence not be forgotten.

We may dry up many sources of crime by education, and by the same means may lessen the amount of sorrow and lengthen life. Here, surely, are good wages to be had for good work : we may,—

Drain the Swamps and increase the Bridges.